Renting

for

dummies®

A Wiley Brand

Renting

by Abdul Muid

Renting For Dummies®

Published by: **John Wiley & Sons, Inc.**, 111 River Street, Hoboken, NJ 07030-5774, www.wiley.com

Copyright © 2024 by John Wiley & Sons, Inc., Hoboken, New Jersey

Published simultaneously in Canada

For general information on our other products and services, please contact our Customer Care Department within the U.S. at 877-762-2974, outside the U.S. at 317-572-3993, or fax 317-572-4002. For technical support, please visit https://hub.wiley.com/community/support/dummies.

Wiley publishes in a variety of print and electronic formats and by print-on-demand. Some material included with standard print versions of this book may not be included in e-books or in print-on-demand. If this book refers to media such as a CD or DVD that is not included in the version you purchased, you may download this material at http://booksupport.wiley.com. For more information about Wiley products, visit www.wiley.com.

Library of Congress Control Number: 2023951078

ISBN 978-1-119-91297-2 (pbk); ISBN 978-1-119-91299-6 (ebk); ISBN 978-1-119-91298-9 (ebk)

SKY10062891_121823

Contents at a Glance

Table of Contents

Introduction

Are you ready to embark on the journey of finding your dream rental? The search for a new home can be a roller coaster of emotions, but the ride becomes smoother when you're armed with the correct information.

Whether you're a first-time renter, new to your city or state, or just in need of a refresher, *Renting For Dummies* is your go-to guide. This book takes you through the essential steps, from understanding income requirements and credit ratings to finding the perfect rental agent and beyond. It's all about removing the guesswork and allowing you to find your new home efficiently and easily. Welcome to the world of stress-free renting! I'm happy to take this journey with you.

About This Book

Renting For Dummies is a comprehensive guide born from my years of experience as a seasoned real estate broker. In this book, I personally walk you through the step-by-step process of finding your ideal rental property, acing your application, and making a seamless transition to your new home.

This book offers valuable nuggets to help you find your perfect rental home in any market. I get into the nitty-gritty details, such as understanding the documentation property owners require for their due diligence. Using this book as your guide significantly improves your chances of success in your renting journey, whether you're eyeing a single-family home, a multifamily residence, a cozy condo, a cooperative apartment, or a place in a sprawling high-rise building.

Throughout the book, I help you craft the perfect application, share tips on working with property managers, identify your lease's vital role, provide expert advice on setting up your utilities, and guide you on securing an easy security deposit return when you're ready to move on. I also give you strategies for increasing the odds of getting application approval and securing a lease renewal.

My extensive hands-on experience working closely with landlords and renters sets this book apart. Enhancing the lives of those I collaborate with is an integral part of my mission. Driven by the desire to help people achieve their real estate dreams, my journey in real estate began after a successful stint in the insurance industry. Fast-forward several years, and I'm still dedicated to that mission.

A quick note: The Technical Stuff icon and sidebars (shaded boxes of text) dig into the details of a given topic, but they aren't crucial to understanding it. Feel free to read them or skip them.

Also, within this book, you may note that some web addresses break across two lines of text. If you're reading this book in print and want to visit one of these web pages, simply key in the web address exactly as it appears in the text, pretending as though the line break doesn't exist. If you're reading this as an e-book, you've got it easy — just click the web address to be taken directly to the web page.

Foolish Assumptions

Here are some assumptions I make about you, dear reader, and why you're picking up this book:

>> You're new to your location and need to find the right home, and you don't know where to start.

>> You're a first-time renter looking for your new home in a competitive rental market.

>> You've lived in your current place for ages and have no idea what it takes to find a rental these days.

>> You're a busy professional with little time to devote to finding your rental. You want an easily digestible guide to help you accomplish your goal easily and quickly.

Icons Used in This Book

Like all *For Dummies* books, this book features icons to help you navigate the information. Here's what they mean:

If you take away anything from this book, make it the information marked with this icon.

REMEMBER

A Technical Stuff icon flags information that delves a little deeper than usual into different facets of renting and real estate.

TECHNICAL STUFF

This icon highlights especially helpful advice about finding and moving into a rental.

TIP

The Warning icon points out situations and actions to avoid on your renting journey.

WARNING

Beyond the Book

In addition to the material in the print or e-book you're reading right now, this product comes with some access-anywhere goodies on the web. Check out the free Cheat Sheet for info on documents you need to apply for a rental, important terms in a lease, and more. To get this Cheat Sheet, simply go to www. dummies.com and search for "*Renting For Dummies* Cheat Sheet" in the Search box.

Where to Go from Here

By design, you don't have to read a *For Dummies* book cover to cover. That said, if you want to master finding your dream rental and have time on your side, I encourage you to read the entire thing.

If the thought of signing a lease is overwhelming, head to Chapter 6, which breaks down the common parts of the lease. After you've secured a place, Parts 3 and 4 can help you make it a home. You can always check out the table of contents and the index for specific topics, too. Good luck!

1
Getting Started with Renting

Begin your journey to finding your next home. Figure out where to start and find out some important truths about renting.

Identify the amenities you want and need in your next rental.

Understand that your budget and preferences come into play when choosing a property and a neighborhood. Consider options such as a full-service building, a private house, or a building with a door person.

Chapter **1**

Understanding the Truths of Renting

The day you sign a lease on a new apartment or house can sometimes feel like the beginning of a relationship. You and the property owner have committed to trust, transparency, respect, and keeping your word to honor the lease.

Maintaining your commitment to paying your rent on time, being a great neighbor, and keeping your home in tiptop shape are a few essential steps to being an excellent tenant.

Likewise, a landlord is committed to responding to your inquiries promptly and efficiently and always maintaining a professional and respectful rapport with you.

This chapter helps you get started with having a happy renting experience.

REMEMBER

When you're searching for a place to call home, note that such a home can come in many different shapes and sizes. Some people rent an entire house, some rent an apartment, and some rent a room or floor in a private house.

Comparing Renting a Place to Buying a Home

Why should you consider renting rather than buying a home? The upfront cost is the most significant difference between the two options:

>> Home purchases sometimes require a down payment of 20 percent of the purchase price. Then you add on the closing costs, which are usually 3 to 5 percent of the purchase price.

TECHNICAL STUFF

You can qualify for a Federal Housing Administration (FHA) loan if you're a first-time home buyer. An FHA loan allows you to make a lower down payment of 3 to 5 percent of the purchase price rather than the standard 20 percent.

>> As a renter, on the other hand, your upfront cost is the first month's rent, security deposit, and broker fee if you use the services of a licensed real estate agent.

Here's how that breaks down for purchasing a $400,000 home:

>> A down payment of 20 percent equals $80,000.

>> At 3 percent, closing costs are an additional $12,000; at 5 percent, that jumps to $20,000.

>> Added together, your upfront costs are between $92,000 and $100,000.

Upfront rental costs vary by market, but they'll almost certainly run much less than $100,000 for a similar property.

TIP

Consult with a mortgage professional to run the numbers if you're considering buying a home versus renting.

Getting an Overview of the Rental Process

Ready to rent? Great! The following sections cover the general steps of the rental process, from deciding which amenities you want in a home to signing the lease, paying the upfront costs, and moving in.

Also, I discuss some of the best apps to search for your home and how to ensure your application is approved.

Figuring out what you want in your new home

REMEMBER

When starting on your journey to find your rental, you may not know what kind of space you're looking for. And guess what? It's okay; finding a place to call home is a learning process. Don't get discouraged; get out and look at places. The more you explore and see, the more you understand what you don't want and what makes one space better for you than another. This process helps you discover what you love.

To figure out what you want in your new home, start with the amenities you must (or really, really want to) have.

>> Does washing dishes bore you? You should include a dishwasher on your must-have list.

>> Do you prefer to do your laundry in the privacy of your home? You may need an in-unit washer and dryer.

>> Does the idea of having private outdoor space excite you? You may need to include outdoor space on your list.

Also think about the charm and aesthetic. Are you a wood floor lover? Do you like high ceilings? Do you prefer a modern or a pre-war look? You get my point.

Now, get your pen and pad and make notes about what you want and what appeals to you. Your home should reflect you; it should exhibit your personality. When you truly live well, those boxes are checked off.

See Chapter 2 for more about figuring out which amenities you want in a rental home. Chapter 3 has details on considering different types of buildings and neighborhoods.

Searching high and low for the perfect place

Looking for the ideal place usually begins on the right app or website. Many good websites and rental apps can help you find your new home. Here are a couple of the options:

» One of my personal favorites is realtor.com (www.realtor. com). It's a national site that allows you to search for apartments in your favorite neighborhoods. Wherever you're looking, the platform is easy to navigate; gives you the contact details for the landlord's agent; and prominently displays the bedroom and bathroom count, the price, and a map that shows similar properties in the surrounding area.

Just as important, it pulls from multiple databases with reliable sources to ensure that you get the most accurate and up-to-date information.

» Another reliable source to search is Homes.com (www.homes. com). This platform is straightforward to use; provides large images of the properties; and allows you to search by entering the neighborhood, agent, school, or place.

The real estate agent's contact details and the answers to the most critical questions about the unit and property are on the main page and not hidden on the last screen of the listing details.

Keep in mind that when you work with a licensed real estate agent, they have access to the best listing platforms to ensure that you have access to all the available properties for rent. Chapter 4 has details on searching for properties and working with a rental agent.

When embarking on your search for a new home, making time to see all the listings as soon as possible increases your odds of finding your ideal home.

Applying to rent a space

You're employed, have a strong credit rating with excellent on-time payments, have 6 to 12 months of rent saved, have gathered all the important documents you need, and make an income 40 times the asking rent. In other words, you're ready to apply for your future rental home!

REMEMBER

When you apply for a rental, the most crucial factor to keep in mind is to make sure you can paint a picture of your ability to pay the rent. You can show your verified income through your offer letter, pay stubs, W-9, or tax returns. Discuss with your rental agent or the rental's property manager the documents required to submit your application.

Getting approved for a rental says your application has demonstrated to the property manager or landlord that you're qualified to pay the rent. Nothing can stop you!

Chapter 5 has the full scoop on applying to rent your dream rental home.

Signing the lease and paying upfront costs

You've made it to the lease signing. The upfront cost at this stage is generally the first month's rent and your security deposit, which can be one- or one-and-a-half-months' rent, and any broker fee, if you're using a broker.

REMEMBER

The security deposit amount varies depending on the state you live in and the landlord you're renting from. The broker fee also varies; some fees can range between 10 and 15 percent of the annual rent or a fee equivalent to one month's rent.

Depending on the type of building you move into, you may need to pay additional upfront moving fees, such as the following:

>> A pet fee or deposit

>> A building-related administrative fee

>> A parking fee

>> An elevator fee

REMEMBER

The preceding fees are generally associated with larger apartment buildings. Rental buildings with ten or fewer units and private rental homes don't usually charge move-in fees. The first month's rent and security deposit are the most these properties typically expect you to pay.

Speak with your property manager, rental agent, or landlord about the fees in advance. Some may be refundable. You can usually pay all fees due at lease signing by certified check, credit card, or electronic payment.

See Chapter 6 for details on signing your lease and paying the necessary fees. Chapter 11 has the scoop on renewing your lease.

Moving and settling in

Moving can bring new renters excitement, joy, and even anxiety. The prospect of working around empty boxes sprawled out, renting a moving truck, or hiring movers can be daunting. Don't fret; with preparation and organization, you'll be all packed in no time.

REMEMBER

Settling into your new home can take a few days or months. Often the most organized and detail-oriented renters unpack and settle in right away so they can return to their usual way of doing things. For some movers, however, settling happens piece by piece, and they unpack when they can. One way isn't better than the other. It all comes down to your preference or timeline.

Settling in can sometimes mean getting to know your door attendant, figuring out where the building's gym is, or getting to know your landlord (who also lives in the first-floor apartment of the rental house you're moving in to). Initially, these nuances are part of settling into your new home. Learning them quickly can help your transition and provide an initial sense of comfort.

Whatever feelings moving inspires for you, stay calm, get organized, and break the move down step by step. Chapter 7 can help. You've got this!

Taking on Life in Your Own Apartment or Rental House

Living on your own is freedom. Your home should be your sanctuary. It's where you go to recharge, reflect, and relax. If you've never experienced living on your own, getting your first apartment or rental house may be a pivotal moment in your life — a new beginning or even a coming of age.

The following sections go over some major aspects of living in an apartment or rental house.

Enjoying a range of amenities

Attractive amenities may well have swayed your choice of rental. Essentially, *amenities* encompass those extra features and services a property offers beyond the essential living space. Their purpose is to enrich tenants' lives and set one property apart from others.

What qualifies as an amenity can shift with evolving trends and tenant preferences, but the following list highlights several amenities that may exist in your rental:

>> **Fitness facilities:** On-site gyms, fitness centers, or yoga studios are popular apartment building amenities that provide an outlet for health-conscious tenants.

>> **Co-working spaces:** As remote work continues to become more common, apartment buildings offering co-working spaces or business centers can attract tenants who need a place to work outside their apartments.

>> **Common areas:** Spaces such as lounges, rooftop terraces, and green spaces provide tenants with places to connect and relax with neighbors.

>> **In-unit laundry:** Having a washer and dryer within the rental is a highly desired amenity because it saves tenants the hassle of going to a communal laundry facility.

>> **Bike storage:** Especially in an apartment building, providing storage for bikes and even bike repair stations caters to environmentally conscious tenants and cycling enthusiasts.

>> **Pet services:** Some rentals offer amenities like dog parks, pet washing stations, and pet day-care services for tenants with pets.

>> **Package lockers:** Dedicated areas for easy, safe delivery of packages have become a valuable amenity.

>> **Innovative home features:** Some properties are equipped with smart home technology, such as keyless entry, smart thermostats, and home automation systems.

>> **Swimming pools:** Whether indoor or outdoor, pools can be a desirable feature, especially in warmer climates.

The ideal amenities can transform your living space far beyond what you imagined. For example, full-service apartment buildings create an environment that tends to every facet of your life.

As you navigate your rental choices, take a moment to assess the perks various amenities bring, ensuring that they harmonize with your individual preferences and budget and enhance your living experience.

REMEMBER

Amenities often come hand in hand with slightly higher rental costs, but I believe the convenience they bring and their potential to elevate your overall living experience are worth considering. Depending on your budget, the premium attached to living in an amenities-rich building may be a wise investment. See Chapter 2 for more information on considering the amenities you want in a rental.

TIP

Don't forget about things to do in your neighborhood! Choosing a neighborhood with a healthy number of amenities is a plus. Your neighborhood is your community, and connecting with the things that help define it is good. Some of the most desirable neighborhoods offer great parks, restaurants, cultural venues, and more, so if your budget allows it, make sure your new neighborhood offers things you're drawn to. Flip to Chapter 3 for more details.

Living in peace with your neighbors

Whatever kind of rental you live in, getting to know your neighbors can be a good thing. It gives you comfort in knowing you have someone who can alert you of an emergency or even just any changes in the building or procedures. Some neighbors exchange keys with each other to keep themselves from getting locked out.

In a time when people are building more and more relationships virtually versus in person, your neighbors can connect you with other neighbors or people in the wider community that may enhance your life.

Chapter 9 has full details on how to live peacefully with neighbors, whether you're in an apartment building or a rental house. Chapter 12 covers following the rules and staying safe when you live in close quarters with others.

A PERK OF APARTMENT LIVING: (POSSIBLY) HAVING A DOOR PERSON

One benefit of living in an apartment building — as opposed to a rental house — is having a door person. (Keep in mind, though, that not all apartment buildings employ one.) Your door person

- Helps keep your apartment building safe and secure
- Ensures that authorized guests and delivery people gain access to the building
- Keeps the lobby clear of hazards
- Alerts you to anything happening in the building
- Is sometimes the designated person to receive an essential item

In short, they're there to help make your life easier.

The relationship with your door person should be one of respect, care, and professionalism. Your door person is your friend. During the end-of-year holidays, residents customarily tip the door person. Especially if door people do their job well, they appreciate tipping and can sometimes earn a large percentage of their earnings from it.

Working with a property manager

Property managers often take on managing a property that the owner doesn't live near or doesn't want to handle personally. A *property manager* is an individual or entity the property owner hires to oversee and, well, manage the daily workings of their real estate property.

Property manager responsibilities can include the following:

>> Setting and collecting rent

>> Handling maintenance requests

>> Filling vacant units

>> Creating a budget for the property

Depending on the owner's needs, a property manager can be one person or a management company. Either way, your property manager's role is to ensure that the place runs smoothly. That includes receiving tenant notifications about issues in their homes and, for apartments, in or around the building.

The property manager is your first contact when you have a problem in your rental. For example, you should reach out to your property manager if your appliances stop working, if you have an electrical or plumbing problem, if your roof leaks, or if you see a hazard around your apartment building.

Making them aware as soon as the problem arises is important. Most property managers want to address issues as quickly as possible to minimize the cost of repair.

Note: Most property managers work standard business hours (9 a.m. to 5 p.m.). If you call after those hours, you may get an operator to record and report your issue to the property manager, who will call you back.

See Chapter 10 for details on working well with a property manager.

Considering maintenance, repairs, and decor

Renting a property offers the advantage of alleviating concerns over maintenance and repairs because those are the owner's responsibility. However, you have to do your part in maintaining the property. That involves not only keeping the living space tidy but also using it in a way that prevents any avoidable damage or harm beyond normal *wear and tear* (the expected deterioration of items because of regular use). The owner is typically obligated to replace items that have exceeded their manufacturer-recommended life span.

Generally speaking, when repairs are necessary — for instance, if the dishwasher malfunctions — quickly notify your property manager or landlord. They coordinate with a service provider to evaluate the damage and proceed with the needed repairs.

For apartment buildings specifically, you may encounter a couple of different scenarios depending on the size of the building:

>> In smaller buildings, tenants may be able (with prior approval from the landlord) to directly hire a repair person and pay the repair cost themselves. In these instances, they can then submit the receipts or invoices and have the incurred expenses deducted from the rent.

>> In larger buildings, you should first contact the landlord or property manager regarding repairs. From there, they take charge of the repair process, arranging necessary appointments with service providers. Tenants in larger complexes aren't required to make any direct payments for repairs.

Tenants are generally not obligated to cover repair costs unless explicitly stated in the lease agreement.

REMEMBER

Familiarize yourself with the policies outlined in your lease agreement (which I cover in Chapter 6) and promptly communicate any maintenance or repair concerns. See Chapter 10 for details on what to do when something goes wrong in your rental.

TIP

Also make sure that your lease spells out the cosmetic changes and upgrades you're allowed to make in your rental. Being intentional about designing a home that reflects your lifestyle can be inspiring and welcoming to you and your guests. You get to decide what style works for you and the furnishings that fit in the space to provide comfort, texture, and warmth. See Chapter 13 for details.

Renting Space in a Private House

Renting space in a private house occurs less frequently than renting an entire apartment or house (I cover those options in the earlier section "Taking on Life in Your Own Apartment or Rental House"). However, the right fit provides you with some benefits.

REMEMBER

Make sure you conduct due diligence to determine whether the city or town allows you to rent this kind of place. Zoning laws may prohibit anyone from renting space within a private residence.

Before committing to this kind of rental, carefully consider the entire scenario. The following sections can help.

REMEMBER Be aware that you're renting space within a private house and sharing everything in the home. Living in close quarters with the owner can be harmonious and peaceful, or sometimes awkward and cumbersome. These arrangements can be affordable and provide flexible lease terms, but you give up some of your privacy.

REMEMBER Like with any other kind of rental, your lease agreement should spell out the monthly rent, security deposit, utility payment, and other essential details such as late fees, house rules, and the lease expiration date. How you and the landlord split the utilities in this situation can vary (50/50, included in the rent, and so on). Request a copy of the utility bills to confirm what you're paying. (See Chapter 8 for details on paying utilities and other expenses beyond rent.)

Living with your landlord: Pros and cons

Yes, living with your landlord is a thing. In most multifamily homes in U.S. cities, the landlord rents out a portion of their home. For instance, many of my clients live on a floor or two of a house and rent the remaining floors for additional income.

Some renters look for homes with an owner as the occupant. This setup gives the renter an added level of security and comfort. They get to live in a quiet, well-maintained building. They find comfort in knowing the owner can quickly address any concerns or issues with the building and rented space. (Most owner-occupants are responsive to problems right away because they understand that taking care of an issue immediately may save money.)

TIP Another benefit is having someone who's lived in the area and can recommend the best local restaurants and shops.

WARNING If you prefer to come and go as you like, host as many guests as possible, and have a more active and entertaining lifestyle, living with your landlord in part of their house may not be the ideal situation for you. Your coming in late when the landlord is sleeping may disrupt their sleep habits and become a situation. (This warning goes the other way, too; living with a landlord who wants to party long after you've gone to bed probably isn't going to be an idyllic home life.)

Just knowing that they're living with the landlord can make some renters feel like they have to walk on eggshells. You're likely going to see your landlord daily, even during awkward or contentious periods. Or perhaps you have a landlord who complains or nit-picks about every minor situation, such as leaving the mail in the mailbox or an item at the front door for too long. Whether their reminders are just annoying or actively passive-aggressive, this kind of potential interaction is something you need to consider.

Being mindful

REMEMBER

Especially when you're sharing a private home with multiple floors, monitoring your sounds, steps, and conversation tone is an important part of neighborly courtesy. These small gestures go a long way toward a peaceful home environment. Chapter 9 has more details on being a thoughtful neighbor.

Being a mindful neighbor in this kind of rental scenario goes beyond just not acting like a jerk. If your landlord is elderly, consider offering to help carry their groceries. Perform random acts of kindness, such as baking cookies or giving flowers. When the homeowner is considering your lease renewal, they're going to think about whether you're a tenant who's respectful, professional, and caring.

TIP

When hosting guests in this kind of rental, be considerate and give your landlord a heads-up, particularly if you anticipate the gathering lasting into the night. If you have a great rapport with the landlord, you may even want to consider inviting them, too.

Contacting your landlord when necessary

REMEMBER

The million-dollar question is always "When do you contact your landlord?"

>> In case of an emergency, whether that's a fire, a leak, an electrical issue, or something else you think the landlord should be aware of as soon as possible.

>> When your stove breaks, your dishwasher stops working, or if you have a clogged bathtub. Most responsive landlords want to know immediately when something breaks or needs repair. The sooner they're aware of problems, the better. Issues or repairs that linger can cost more to repair, so timely reporting saves money.

The lease signing is a great time to discuss what's considered an emergency and when you should contact the landlord. Most communications should occur during regular business hours, such as 8 a.m. to 6 p.m. or 9 a.m. to 5 p.m. In some instances and emergencies, you must contact your landlord after business hours, however. The lease will also contain language in the lease to cover these situations. For more information on getting help when things go wrong in your rental, head to Chapter 10.

Chapter **2**

Evaluating Your Rental Hopes and Realities

What does a dream rental look like to you? Does it have lots of natural light, an eat-in kitchen, built-in bookshelves, a lovely terrace, or something else? But here's an even more important question to ask yourself: Can you have your dream rental in reality?

In this chapter, I identify the essential elements your rental home needs to ensure that you experience comfort and happiness throughout your stay. Just as important, I help you do the math to determine the amount of monthly rent you can afford and show you the key things landlords look at to make sure you don't get in over your head.

TIP

Perhaps you know exactly when you want to move into an apartment or a rental house. If so, start looking at possible places online (see Chapter 4) and pulling all the paperwork together (see Chapter 5). But if the idea of moving is still just that — an idea — your first step is determining when you want to move. Spring is the most active time of the year to find a new apartment or rental house. On average, finding a home that feels good to you takes 30 to 60 days.

Considering What You Want from a Rental

REMEMBER

Most people want their home to be a sanctuary. They want a place where they can unwind without being bothered by neighbors or distracted by noises from highway traffic or blaring sirens. When embarking on your search for a new home, consider asking the following questions:

» What type of energy do I want in my home?

» What key elements of living am I drawn to?

» How much room do I need?

» Do I want the space and the surrounding building/ neighborhood to be quiet?

Choosing the right home can be the difference between a calm, productive life filled with happy moments and a life filled with low energy, chaos, and hardly memorable times. Many things contribute to whether you love a rental or can't wait to get out of it, such as the following:

» Sound levels

» Natural light and the views out your windows

» Amount of living space

» Proximity to shopping, restaurants, activities, and your job

» The amenities that the complex or neighborhood offers

These critical elements of a happy lifestyle allow an abundance of creativity, peace, and focus. The following sections offer up food for thought on all these topics.

Building style: Old, new, or something in between?

If you're someone who covets old-world charm and all things historic, then an older property may be your top choice. The charm and character these types of places offer makes them fun to live in. The original floors, walls, and decorative fireplaces add so much character and often become talking points at your dinner parties.

However, older buildings have their drawbacks. Older apartment buildings may or may not have elevators. The appliances and fixtures may be ten (or more) years old. If they have air conditioning, it's usually a window unit, which may not cool the entire place but still be expensive. Older buildings can be in great neighborhoods, but they can also be in questionable ones.

If your style leans toward modern and trendy, then you likely want to check out the newest apartment complexes or rental homes in the area. They have all the bells and whistles: smart thermostats, walk-in closets, fireplaces, bike storage areas, package rooms, and more. Maybe you'll use all those features, or maybe you'll use only a handful. But keep in mind that you pay for those amenities regardless of whether you use them. You get to decide whether the cost is worth it.

New apartment complexes and rental houses have their own shortcomings. The walls, floors, and ceilings may be so thin that you can hear your neighbor walking above you in their own apartment or the neighbor in the house next door sneeze. The demand is usually strong for areas with the latest and greatest amenities, so you may need to get on a waiting list to rent there. New rentals can also be expensive compared to similar older rentals in the area, so you need to have a good grasp of your housing budget. (See the later section "Running the Numbers to See What You Can Afford" for more information.)

If you're looking for historic charm with modern finishes, then a marriage of the two may be a great fit for you. Often, landlords search far and wide to purchase an old building with tons of charm just to give it a makeover, blending all the original architectural elements with shiny new updated kitchens, bathrooms, walls, and floors. They offer modern comforts such as washers and dryers, stainless steel appliances, central heat and air, radiant heated floors, spa-like tubs, and much more. They also generally price these spaces at a premium.

If your budget doesn't allow new and shiny but you still want mostly renovated, then an apartment or house renovated within the last five to seven years is your perfect match. This type of space should offer nice options at affordable prices.

TIP

If you opt for a rental that fits your budget but is short on the aesthetic you're after, you can create the look and feel you want with creative styling and appropriate furniture (see Chapter 13). What's just as important is to consider what you're drawn to, or what immediately speaks to your heart as soon as you walk through the door. This approach ensures that you have a joyful stay.

Determining how much space you need

Before committing to your new home, figure out how much space will allow you to live a happy, productive life. You need room for everyone you plan to have live with you (two-legged and four-legged), but you also need room for all your stuff.

People and lifestyle

Consider how many people will be living in the rental. You alone? You and your teenaged kid(s)? You and a sibling or roommate? Each of those examples likely requires different sleeping arrangements, so you need to be sure about how many bedrooms you need.

Then you want to think about other space. Are you going to throw a party every weekend for a dozen friends or keep your privacy and solitude pretty tight? That influences how much kitchen and living room space you want. Are you going to work from home? If so, do you want a designated room for your office, or can you work from the kitchen table or a corner of your bedroom? Consider the many ways you can use living space and make sure your future home is conducive to your lifestyle.

Furniture

Having an idea of the sizes of common pieces of furniture can help you gauge how much space your stuff takes up in relation to room dimensions. A king- or queen-size bed require at least a 10-foot-x-10-foot space. A medium to large couch requires a room with two walls measuring at least 8 feet in width. Your dining space needs at least a 7-foot-x-7-foot space to fit a table. These details are important to know (or find out) as your fine-tune your search.

The average one-bedroom apartment can range from small to large and approximately 500 to 800 square feet. Having an accurate floor plan helps you gauge what you're potentially working with. A good floor plan provides the dimensions of the rooms, halls, kitchen, and bathroom(s). An exceptional floor plan provides the dimensions of the closets and the ceiling height.

TIP

If you have a special item that's rather large (like a pinball machine or 75-inch flat-screen TV) that you want to put in your rental, make sure the place has space for it. Note the item's measurements on your phone and compare those to the floor plan. Or take a tape measure with you when you view the unit and get a rough idea of whether the piece will fit the space. (Chapter 4 has more details on touring properties.)

Amenities: Luxurious, scant, or middle of the road?

Luxury is a word that's used often to imply world-class, top of the line, or, simply put, the best! What's great about this idea is that *you* get to determine what luxury is to you.

Some new buildings offer shiny new apartments with world-class amenities such as gyms with Olympic-size pools and staff, trainers, and masseuses; meeting rooms; door people; party rooms; yoga studios; and even pet spas. Rental houses may be in neighborhoods that have their own playgrounds, tennis and basketball courts, clubhouses, biking trails, and more. These services are often priced into the rent, and therefore you can expect to pay a substantial premium in rent.

Amenities range from run-of-the-mill to "Here, take my deposit." Check out this list of examples:

>> Dishwasher

>> Custom countertops and cabinets, kitchen islands, and stainless-steel appliances

>> Air conditioning

>> High-speed internet access

>> Plush carpet

>> Wood flooring

>> Bark park or doggie day care

>> Balcony or patio, perhaps with outdoor storage

>> Spa

- Swimming pool
- Fitness center
- Rooftop deck
- In-unit washer and dryer
- Laundry facility
- Valet trash collection
- Garage
- Covered parking
- Bike storage
- Gated access
- Package lockers
- Electric car charging stations
- Smart locks, thermostats, or appliances
- Movie theater or screening room
- Community rooms
- Putting green
- Common areas with grills and playgrounds
- On-site restaurant or coffee shop

You may look at items on this list and think, "That's not an amenity." But when you're doing laundry for a family of four, having an in-unit washer and dryer is something you appreciate with every load of clothes. Sure, having a laundry room in the building or on the property is almost as good, but if you need to wash the toddler's sheets at 3 a.m., you'll be thankful to have a washing machine in your home.

REMEMBER

Many nice rentals don't have these bells and whistles. When your budget doesn't allow for luxurious amenities, choosing an unrenovated and well-maintained residence may be an excellent fit. Often this type of rental is priced below the market average and can provide you great value. Be sure that the space is clean and maintained well.

Commute times and convenience

Your commute to and from work is important when considering where you live. Start with your lifestyle. Do you want the flexibility of leaving work late and stopping at a local bar or restaurant for dinner and drinks? Does the idea of making long drives and being stuck in traffic give you heart palpitations? If so, a shorter commute time is great for you. If you believe a quiet commute in your car is fulfilling and rewarding, a longer commute may be your best choice.

Budget can also be a factor in your commute time. You pay more to rent in an area everyone wants to live in; if you work in one of those areas and have a modest budget, you may need to look at renting in a less expensive area and taking a longer commute. This way, you're saving money by paying a lower rent.

Another critical element to consider is whether you drive or take public transportation (if it's available in your area). Think about the cost of monthly parking and gas versus a monthly commuter pass on the train or bus. A public-transportation or carpool commute can give you time to catch up on work, reading, and doing other miscellaneous tasks that a driving commute doesn't.

Consider being in close proximity to everyday conveniences like the grocery store, gas station (if you have a car), a park, a dog run, and a good school for your child. Do keep in mind there is usually a premium or higher rent you pay to be near these must-have amenities.

REMEMBER

Just be sure to consider which approach has the best impact on your life in the long term.

Party city or a quiet area?

Surrounding living environments can range from high-intensity to low-key. Depending on your ideal fit, both types can be peaceful.

An apartment complex with a party vibe mostly offers you a younger demographic along with convenience and access to nightlife. Generally speaking, your neighbors will be a few years removed from college, such as single professionals who prefer a vibrant, on-the-go lifestyle. This kind of environment typically has bars, restaurants, shopping, multiple grocery store options, a transportation hub, and parks.

A quiet apartment complex or neighborhood can provide the opposite atmosphere — an older, more stable demographic and young and older families, all looking for calm, serenity, and less hustle and bustle. In a quiet area, you find fewer rental apartments. Instead, these communities have mostly single-family homes or small complexes without stores, restaurants, or shopping districts.

Running the Numbers to See What You Can Afford

REMEMBER

If you're renting your first place, or renting for the first time in many years, you may be shocked at rental prices. People across the country and in every economic bracket are always surprised at the cost of rent. People tend to think of apartments in particular as "just a building," but so much more goes into that building: maintenance and repairs, upgrades or renovations, staff costs, landscaping, utilities, insurance, taxes, advertising, and so on.

All those costs add up fast, and each renter benefits from those expenses. So each renter in an apartment building shares in the cost of paying for them in the form of rent. The following sections help you figure out how much rent you can afford and which other expenses you need to factor into your budget, whether you're renting an apartment or a house.

Sizing up your salary

Your salary is one of the most important pieces of the rental puzzle. How much you earn per month determines what you should pay toward your living expense. It's also a major factor in determining whether you're approved, because it's how the landlord determines their risk. The higher your salary, the better the odds the landlord will approve you as a tenant. (Find out more about this topic in the later section "Understanding How Landlords Determine Your Eligibility").

TIP

If you haven't created a budget that lists all your expenses, now is a good time to do that. Grab a piece of paper or pull up a spreadsheet and list everything you already spend money on in a month or will need to pay for if you're going out on your own: groceries, cellphone bill, car payment, credit card bills, streaming services, student loan payment, and so on.

Add up all those expenses and subtract them from your monthly take-home salary. That number indicates what you have left for rent.

WARNING

If you're spending 45 to 50 percent of your earnings toward rent, stop! You're paying too much. As I explain later in this chapter, the ideal max is 30 percent of your earnings, but a comfortable percentage that allows you to save, and to enjoy life, is about 20 percent.

If you don't like the number you see or think it's too small, you need to make some adjustments. You can

>> Cut some expenses

>> Find a way to supplement your income

>> Consider looking for a cheaper place to live

Factoring in costs beyond rent

When you're determining your costs, you must remember to calculate related housing expenses that aren't part of the rent. These can include costs like the following:

>> Electricity

>> Heat

>> Water

>> Wi-Fi

>> Your building's gym fee (if you're choosing an apartment building)

>> Parking fee (if applicable)

>> Renter's insurance

REMEMBER

These charges are things you pay monthly in addition to your base rent. So don't forget to allocate funds for these expenses. Go back and add them to the budget that you may have created in the preceding section.

Understanding How Landlords Determine Your Eligibility

What you think you can afford to pay for a rental and what industry experts recommend may be two different things. And the landlord's opinion is what matters.

Your salary, credit rating, savings, and debt-to-income ratio are major factors landlords use to determine your eligibility. Most landlords look at your earnings and figure that about 30 percent of that should go toward your housing expense. Steady employment is also a plus; the longer you've been employed, the more comfort the landlord has with choosing you as their new tenant. But other factors may come into play to determine your eligibility, as you find out in the following sections.

Help from a few important documents

When you find your dream apartment or house, the landlord requests multiple documents, including your most recent credit report, to determine your eligibility as well as (see Chapter 5 for full details). Here's an introduction to some of the most important info you have to provide:

>> **Employment verification letter:** An *employment verification letter* verifies your hire date, your title, and your annual salary. It's on company letterhead and includes the name and contact number of an official within the company to verbally verify your employment. Your HR department can provide this letter.

TIP

Are you paid weekly, biweekly, or once a month? In the rare case you're paid once a month, the landlord may verify the date funds are available in your account every month to make the rent payments. They may also require you may to pay rent by electronic withdrawals on the determined date.

If you're self-employed, instead of an employment verification letter, you may be able to provide a profit-and-loss statement from your accountant, tax returns for your business, and bank account statements in addition to a credit report and a landlord reference letter.

>> **Credit report:** Your *credit report* shows your history of making on-time payments, how long you've maintained your

monthly revolving credit lines, and your total debt obligations. (*Revolving credit* is the kind that replenishes after you pay it off. Credit cards are a common example of revolving credit.)

Your credit score is important too. The higher your score, the more favorable your application. A higher credit score also removes the need for a larger security deposit and a cosigner.

TIP

You should know what's on your credit report before applying for an apartment. Freecreditreport.com offers one annual credit report for free.

TIP

>> **Proof of savings/investments:** Having strong savings and an investment portfolio increases your odds of getting approved. They demonstrate to the landlord that you can pay your bills on time and save money, too. They show that you're in control of your finances and don't spend more than you earn. Your having more liquid assets provides the landlord with additional security that they'll receive their rent on time.

Saving 15 percent of your income per year, including any employer contributions, is an appropriate savings level for many people.

TIP

The 40X-the-rent rule

TIP

The *40X-the-rent* rule is an easy formula to determine how much you should earn in salary to qualify for a given apartment or rental house. Multiply the price of the rental by the number 40.

For example, say the price of your new dream home is $2,000 per month. Multiply that number by 40 to find your target salary:

$2,000 × 40 = $80,000

Your salary should be no less than $80,000 to qualify for the apartment. That's a fast and easy way to make sure you qualify.

REMEMBER

Some landlords may approve applications that fall below the 40X amount. I've seen this scenario with tenants who have excellent savings/investments, solid references, and impeccable payment history on their credit reports and who had a strong one-on-one meeting with the landlord.

The 30 percent rule

TIP

The *30 percent rule* says that you should allocate no more than 30 percent of your earnings toward your monthly housing expense. The idea is to ensure that you have 70 percent of your income to dedicate to other expenses.

To determine your target amount, multiply your annual salary by 30 percent. For example, say $100,000 is your annual salary. (I'm using this number just to make the math here easy.)

$100,000 × 30 percent = $30,000

You can afford $30,000 a year to cover your housing expenses. Now divide $30,000 by 12 months in a year.

$30,000 ÷ 12 = $2,500

You can afford to pay $2,500 per month in rent. (If you find a place you love for even less, that's great news!)

Your debt-to-income ratio

Your *debt-to-income* (DTI) ratio is an important part of your financial health. It compares how much debt you have to how much income you have.

When you apply for your rental, your landlord evaluates your debt-to-income ratio to help determine the risk associated with your taking on the rent for your new home. Therefore, a lower debt-to-income ratio is ideal — and improves your odds of getting the place. See how to calculate your debt-to-income ratio in a couple of simple steps:

1. **Add up your monthly bills.**

    These items may include the following:

    - Monthly rent or house payment
    - Monthly alimony or child support payments
    - Student, auto, and other monthly loan payments
    - Credit card monthly payments (use the minimum payment)
    - Other monthly debt payments

Note: Expenses like groceries and your taxes generally aren't included.

2. **Divide the total by your *gross monthly income,* which is your income before taxes.**

   The result is your DTI ratio, which is a percentage. Ideally, your ratio should be 30 percent or lower.

If you can swing it, eliminate as much debt as you can before submitting an application to rent. The lower your debt-to-income ratio, the less risky you are to your landlord. That increases the chances the landlord approves your application.

Balancing Your Wants with Your Financial Reality

All your expenses and spending activities happen under two categories: your needs and your wants:

>> Your *needs* are things you can't skip without incurring serious consequences. These items include your monthly utility bills, groceries, critical medication, and fuel or transportation. You have to pay for these items first.

>> A *want* is something that improves your life but is ultimately nonessential. Wants include things like the hottest fashion trends and tickets to watch your favorite team. You'd like to have them, but you can also move your life forward without them, even though it may be a little less enjoyable.

Being sure about what you truly need in your home to live happily positively impacts your life. Make a list of items that you must have and stay within that list and your budget. For example, maybe you *want* a woodburning fireplace, skylights, a walk-in closet, and a large soaking tub. Do you *need* these items for a happy lifestyle? Most often, the answer is no. Especially if renting a space with these amenities takes you over your budget, removing them from your list won't hurt your living. You can live happily and be productive in a similar place for less! This situation is a win-win for you.

REMEMBER

Understanding how your wants and needs impact your life positively and negatively is a key element in a happy and productive tenure in a rental property. Think about how often you've made the right choice to stay within your means and the positive impact doing so had.

TIP

In the extreme scenario where you absolutely want to pamper yourself and go over budget, consider one of the following options to make it work:

>> Add a qualified roommate to split the cost. The roommate will need to supply the landlord with the same documentation you do (as I cover earlier in this chapter and in Chapter 5).

>> For an apartment, consider a similar complex with comparable renovations within your budget.

>> Add a side hustle to supplement your income. Make sure that you can verify the income from this side hustle for the landlord.

Chapter **3**

Considering Types of Buildings and Neighborhoods

After you figure out the amenities you need in a space and what you can afford (see Chapter 2), you're ready for the next step in your rental journey. In this chapter, I help you understand why you need to consider the style of building you're drawn to when choosing a new rental home. Your preferences can determine whether you live in a 100-year-old building, an apartment in a private home, a fifth-floor walk-up apartment building, or a new development high-rise building. If your budget allows, you may even consider renting a whole house!

Some neighborhoods are known for their architectural style and the flow of identical facades along with well-kept stoops and yards. Knowing this information beforehand provides you a clear direction on what works best for your lifestyle.

Knowing Different Building Types

Many neighborhoods and communities are defined by the types of buildings they offer.

TIP

How do you know what type of rental is your ideal fit? First, read the following sections for an overview of different building types. Then take a day or two to walk the neighborhoods you're considering. Pay attention to the types of buildings you see in the residential areas. What do you like about them? Also look at the people going in and out of the various building types. What's the energy like? How do you react to that? This practice helps you understand what you're drawn to.

Assessing a building's age

One way to distinguish building types is by age. How old of a building do you want to live in? The following sections cover prewar, postwar, and new apartment buildings.

Prewar buildings

Many mid- and high-rise apartment buildings erected between 1900 and 1939 (before World War II) are considered *prewar.* Prewar apartments are desired for their spaciousness, character and elegance, beautiful hardwood flooring, and tall ceilings. These rare homes offer a peek into the past.

In most prewar buildings, the options range from older and less renovated apartments to fully renovated luxury rentals to spacious co-ops and condominiums (all covered later in this chapter).

If you're part of a growing family or a couple not finding the space you desire in newer, more modern apartments, prewar buildings offer good square footage, value, and pricing. Keep in mind the apartments could be less renovated when compared to newer buildings, but what you get in return, such as large foyers, elegant archways, and generously sized rooms with natural light through large windows, should compensate for it.

Postwar buildings

Postwar buildings were built between World War II and the 1990s. Modern amenities are included, such as central heating and air conditioning, updated plumbing lines, electricity, soundproofing, and insulation. These features increase the efficiency of the building and provide comfort for the occupants.

New buildings

Most newly constructed buildings — anything built within the last five to seven years — offer the latest amenities and technology, including energy-efficient heating and cooling systems, the newest security features, and the fastest internet connections. New buildings are designed to meet or exceed current energy efficiency standards, in turn providing lower utility costs for the residents and a reduced environmental impact. (Buildings from the 1990s and 2000s are considered modern yet older.)

Going beyond landlord-owned apartment buildings

When you rent an apartment, your landlord is typically a person or company that owns the building, and you deal with them directly. But you may discover apartments in buildings that have an unusual ownership structure, like co-ops and condos.

Co-ops

Cooperatives, commonly known as *co-ops*, are apartments in mostly prewar and postwar buildings (which I discuss earlier in this chapter). Co-ops are unique in that people own shares of the corporation that owns the building. These shareholders have a *proprietary lease* (or occupancy agreement) that gives them ownership and use of the apartment.

The co-op has a board that votes on allowing new members to the co-op. That means you submit your application to rent a co-op apartment to the co-op board. The board decides whether you're approved, and the co-op's bylaws dictate the length of your lease.

Choose a co-op if you like the idea of knowing your neighbors and living in an intimate setting, and be ready to be interviewed by the co-op board. But the approval process can be lengthy, and you share most of your finances and personal details with shareholders during the interview process. The co-op sublet policy may limit the length of your lease, sometimes a maximum of two years.

Condominiums

A *condominium* or *condo* is a property in a residential complex of separate units owned by individual owners. Condo owners own just the unit, not the building.

When you rent a condo in a small building — say three to ten units in most cases — you're renting directly from the owner, and the owner approves or denies your application (although some of the smaller buildings have a property management company). You don't have to get board approval. But depending on the number of condo units and the management setup, you may need the condo board or property manager to approve your application.

Condominiums offer more flexible and longer lease terms. The approval process is quicker. But rent prices for condominiums are mostly priced at a premium. Be prepared to pay top dollar to rent one.

Looking at the level of luxury

One typical way to categorize apartment buildings is by the level of luxury they provide. Do you want no-frills basics, something in the middle of the road, or the ultimate in luxury?

Walk-up buildings

A *walk-up building* is a building without an elevator. Translation: You have to walk up actual stairs to your apartment. These buildings are mostly five- or six-story prewar buildings. The amenities for this kind of building are basic. The building may provide a trash compactor chute, a laundry room in the basement, and a superintendent who lives on the premises, but that's about it.

Walk-up buildings usually offer good deals and a good amount of space. However, the lack of elevators and amenities can present a problem for some people.

Elevator buildings

An *elevator building* is an apartment building that provides one or more elevators. They're usually postwar buildings (built mostly during the 1950s to the 1970s) that are at least four stories tall. Some larger buildings even have a separate elevator dedicated to move-in and move-out. Elevator buildings can be large and offer a host of services for your enjoyment, such as a door person, a package room, and other amenities.

An elevator building can provide limited amenities or a host of amenities, but rent prices in elevator buildings are typically higher. If you're looking for more services and amenities while still maintaining affordability, elevator buildings present an attractive option.

Full-service buildings

A *full-service building* is also known as a *luxury building*. It offers first-class service and premium amenities, and the building can be of any age. A few of the benefits you may receive in this kind of building include

>> Door person

>> Gym

>> Pool

>> Package room

>> Media room

>> Valet service

>> Porter

>> Roof deck

>> Yoga studio and/or sauna

>> Indoor parking

TIP

The amenities vary from luxury building to luxury building and don't always include all the preceding services. But the true luxurious full-service buildings go above and beyond to enhance your stay.

If you covet service and world-class amenities, a full service building is an excellent option, but rents in such buildings are out of reach for some people.

Moving past apartments: Single-family homes

A *single-family home* is a home intended for (wait for it) a single family. A single-family home can be free-standing or attached to another home; some provide a driveway, garage, and backyard.

The owner of the single-family home owns the land and the house built on top of it. They approve or deny your application, unless they've hired a property manager who takes on that duty.

A single-family home offers the advantages of privacy, more living space, and private outdoor space. Keep in mind, though, that you could be responsible for some maintenance and upkeep of the property.

Understanding What Distinguishes Neighborhoods

The differences that exist in neighborhoods — and what those mean to you — are key elements to be aware of. Does the area have a thriving dining or downtown scene? What about museums, theaters, galleries, and other cultural attractions? Is there a dog park (or any park)? A transportation hub? Look at the people. What do their movements tell you? Are they walking quickly and with a purpose?

These nuances define most neighborhoods and help give them a distinct feel. Some people choose an active or bustling neighborhood because they want to meet new people and be part of the action. Others choose a quiet neighborhood because they have small children and prefer less hustle and bustle. Paying attention to the considerations in the following sections informs you about the habits of the people and the neighborhood to ensure that you make a good choice for your lifestyle.

TIP

Walking (or driving) around a neighborhood at different times of the day shows you so much about the type of experience you'd have there. What's the Monday morning energy like? How is that different from the 2 p.m. movement? How about the evening? Can you fit in here? Sit down in the coffee shop and pay attention to things that stand out. Are the people friendly? This neighborhood may be yours eventually, too, so make sure it offers the atmosphere you must have. Flip to Chapter 2 for more information on evaluating what you want in a rental home.

You may have gotten a head start on your research while visiting a friend or family member in a particular neighborhood and imagining yourself in that community. Often, choosing a neighborhood just involves closing your eyes and already seeing yourself living and breathing there.

Investigating the price range

Each neighborhood offers things that influence the price of the nearby rentals. Parks, shopping, transportation, restaurants, and a theater or museum add more to the value — and cost — of your place. The demand for the available units can affect the price, too.

Write down the amenities you're sure you want in your new home and neighborhood. Searching for the right price range often requires checking all the amenities boxes when you're researching properties on a search portal. This includes your list of items from your needs list. Doing so allows you to see all the available properties in your price range. Next go a step further and remove all the items off your list to help clarify the reality of price ranges for the available properties in your top neighborhood. Now, do the opposite and check all your desired amenities, but increase your price range on this search. You'll understand the reality of the available properties in your price range. See Chapter 2 for more guidance on establishing your wants and needs.

Checking out neighborhood parks

Parks are often the heartbeat of a neighborhood. So many benefits come with living near a park. It gives the residents of the neighborhood open space and air to relax, exercise, hang out, spend downtime, or walk the dog.

If you have children, parks provide a place to play other than your backyard. Kids get the opportunity to meet other children and make friends. The park becomes an extension of the backyard.

If you have a pet, check to see whether the neighborhood has a dog park. Dog parks let your pet meet and play with other pets and allow you to meet other dog owners.

If these benefits sound good to you, make sure your new neighborhood has or is near a park. Note that apartments next to parks typically rent faster and often come at a premium.

Research has shown a beneficial connection between access to green spaces/parks and happiness and stress levels. Keep your stress low and visit your neighborhood park.

Getting a taste of the restaurant scene

If you love a great restaurant, knowing that a great place to eat exists in your neighborhood is worth its weight in gold. It offers a place to gather, socialize, entertain, and enjoy excellent food.

Getting to know the restaurants in your neighborhood is easy:

>> Start by walking (or driving around) the neighborhood and checking out the design aesthetic of the restaurants' exteriors. Does it look like the proprietors put effort into the design and setup?

>> Look through the window and check to see whether the kitchens are visible. Sometimes a visible kitchen shows freshness and openness and adds value for the eater. However, if you'd rather not know what your meal looked like before it landed in front of you, these restaurants may not work for you. For me, the experience of seeing my food being prepared at a busy restaurant as I'm engulfed in the latest current events is one of the best dining experiences possible, but your mileage may vary.

>> Do the menus specialize in a few dishes done really well, or do they offer a little bit of a lot of things? Do you prefer one of those types of menus to the other?

Be sure that you'll take advantage of the restaurants in a neighborhood. You can expect to pay a premium for living in a neighborhood that offers great restaurant selections, so if you're someone who cooks dinner at home most nights, this kind of neighborhood may not be ideal for you.

Evaluating public transportation (if available)

The joys of public transportation are usually affordable ways to move from Point A to Point B. In some areas, one important feature to consider when picking a neighborhood is the public transportation situation. How can you get to and from your community with and without a car?

Knowing the schedule for buses and train lines is critical. What are the rush-hour or peak times and prices versus the non-rush-hour/off-peak times and prices? You can use the internet to identify the intersections for the buses and trains. Find out how long walking to these locations from your desired neighborhood takes and then actually take the walk. Is it a comfortable journey for you? Determine whether driving to the bus or train and then parking your car is a good option. If so, what's the additional monthly cost you must consider for daily parking?

Alternatively, if you're in a rural or suburban town without major transportation, you should consider how far of a drive or walk matters to you. Think about the proximity to highways and the local roads as a determining factor.

Chapter 2 has more on evaluating what kind of commute time is best for you. Your ideal balance between convenience, time, and cost should factor into your decision when selecting your neighborhood.

Discovering cultural attractions

If you're a fan of live music, are drawn to street art and jazz, or love spending time in museums, culture may be one of the top reasons you're choosing your neighborhood. Discovering local history and culture is an excellent way to spend your time learning more about your favorite neighborhood. Whether you're looking for something fun to do with children, family, or friends, here are a few ideas to get acclimated:

» Look for local tours.

» Visit local galleries and exhibits.

» Go on local hikes.

» Attend local festivals.

Accommodating Fido and Fifi

When I was a kid, we had two cats in our home. The joy of seeing their faces when I arrived home was a moment I looked forward to. Your pets are unique to you, and accommodating them in your new neighborhood requires some due diligence. Therefore, when considering your new home, you should understand the landlord's pet policy beforehand.

Some rentals don't allow pets. Period. Others are pet friendly with some restrictions, such as weight and height limits and caps on the number of pets. Be sure you know the regulations as they pertain to your situation. You may also be required to pay a pet deposit.

Some apartment buildings are pet-friendly and offer pet spas, on-site grooming, day-care options, and partnerships with local groomers, dog walkers, and other pet-based businesses. If you're pet-obsessed and have the budget, these types of buildings are the best options for your pets — I mean, you. I've worked with avid dog owners who chose pet-friendly buildings, and those places were some of the best living experiences they've had.

The ability to live freely with your pet provides you positive energy and freedom. Make sure your building loves your pet, too. See Chapter 9 for more information.

Hunting Down the Perfect Housing

Discover the important first steps in the process of finding your new rental home. Do some legwork, view some properties, and hire a rental agent.

Complete your rental application, one of the most important stages of your approval process.

Understand your lease, its length, and what you must do to uphold its terms.

Chapter **4**

Let the Search Begin!

Your search for a new rental home can be filled with highs and lows, from the disappointment of missing out on that dream place with all the features you want to the joy of finding out your application has been approved after a rigorous search.

Maintaining optimism throughout this journey is critical to achieving success. Stay determined and focused, and persevere until you find your perfect home. This chapter starts you off on the official search.

Warming Up with Some Preliminary Legwork

REMEMBER

Ready to hit the ground running on your rental search? Not so fast! Getting prepared for your search requires asking yourself some questions:

> **» What city or town are you moving to (or within)?**
> Whether it's a local or long-distance move, you can't really search until you know the city and neighborhood you're

considering. Chapter 3 has more about distinguishing different neighborhoods.

» **What's your budget?** Chapter 2 helps you determine what you can afford.

» **What size rental do you want?** A studio apartment? A one- or two-bedroom apartment? Maybe a bigger rental house? Whatever works best for you and your budget, go for it.

» **What amenities do you want or need?** *Want* and *need* are two different concepts. You need a refrigerator; you want a new kitchen with all new appliances. You need a bathroom; you want a fully renovated bath with dual shower heads.

My point is to be aware of the things you truly can't live without and then include these options on your checklist. Keep in mind, though, that the more amenities you have, the more you usually pay in rent. See Chapter 2 for more about amenities.

» **What's your target move-in date?** If your target move-in date is June 1, begin your search on April 15 to give yourself time in case you miss out on a few properties. In tight and competitive rental markets, consider starting your search even earlier.

» **How long a lease are you looking for?** Do you want a one- or two-year lease? Some landlords prefer a one-year lease to start.

» **Do you have a pet?** Some buildings and landlords don't allow pets, so make sure you search for pet-friendly buildings if you have a pet or want the option to get one. See Chapter 9 for more about living in a rental with a pet.

» **Is proximity to public transportation important to you?** If so, remember to identify which train or bus lines are the most convenient for the location(s) you're considering. (Naturally, if you're moving to an area with limited public transportation, you don't need to worry about this issue.)

» **Do you want to work with a rental agent?** Enlisting the expertise of a licensed real estate agent can be a strategic move toward expediting your search and finding a home that aligns with your needs. Find out more about this option in the later section "Working with a Rental Agent."

Compile your answers to these questions, and get ready to get out there and search for your new home with the help of the following sections.

Searching for rentals online

With modern real estate apps, searching for apartments and rental houses online is straightforward. Many real estate platforms actually make searching for a new home fun and engaging. You can view curated professional photos, expertly designed floorplans, and captivating videos that allow you to get intimately familiar with the space before you even set foot inside.

Additionally, most sites have historical pricing data to guide and inform you about average rental prices. You can gather a lot of information about your top neighborhood with a simple swipe or click, which helps ensure that you're making informed choices about your home search.

TIP

Check out the Money Under 30 list of the top real estate websites. Money Under 30 is a personal finance website specializing in financial advice for young adults. Visit www.moneyunder30.com/best-real-estate-websites/ for full details.

Driving or walking around neighborhoods

So you have a few leads on rentals. Great! Before you decide which properties to tour, take a moment to understand the feeling of the place you may call home (if possible). Doing so can help you find a neighborhood that matches what you want.

Driving or walking a neighborhood can give you different perspectives or opinions of the area and a deeper connection to the surroundings. In particular, walking blocks of a neighborhood gives you a closer feel for the people, the community's vitality, and the rich hues of its cultural identity.

REMEMBER

You may already have a head start on this task if you know people in the neighborhood you're considering. When I've asked clients how they learned about a particular area, many have responded, "I have a few friends/relatives/colleagues in the area already, and I've always been drawn to it." Flip to Chapter 3 for more about researching neighborhoods.

Viewing Potential Properties

Looking at properties is the fun part! Each rental has its own unique identity. Now all you have to do is find your match.

Viewing properties in person can be a rewarding and sometimes challenging process. What can make yours easier is having a clear picture of what you want and how you intend to live. Envision your furniture in the space and imagine the sweet smell of your favorite fragrance. Having a strong grasp of what your new home will look and feel like when you see it means you stand a much better chance of knowing immediately when you've found the right place. And nothing beats that feeling.

REMEMBER

Sometimes your search requires you to see all the available rentals in your price range, and sometimes viewing two properties may be all you need.

The following sections give you some pointers on viewing rentals and knowing what to look for.

TIP

Be adventurous and explore. Take in every part of each space you view, walk the neighborhood if you haven't already, and engage with the energy.

TIP

When you settle on properties to look at more closely, also evaluate their locations in relation to important landmarks like your workplace; any public transportation options; and essential amenities like grocery stores, pharmacies, and hospitals. Actually traveling from your workplace to the rental to determine whether this commute makes sense for you is a good practice before signing your lease.

Setting up appointments

Ensuring that you're available to view the properties in person is just as essential as doing the paperwork in finding a new home. As much as possible, make attending property viewings a top priority throughout your home search. Your dedication to attending these viewings means you're committed to finding the perfect home.

TIP

If in-person viewings aren't possible (say you live in a different state and plan to make a long-distance move), don't hesitate to request a video or virtual tour. Many properties offer these options to give you a comprehensive feel of the space.

Contact with the leasing agent, property manager, or individual advertising the space is pivotal. When you come across a property advertisement for the first time, consider this method:

1. **Email the leasing agent through the platform where you found the listing.**

   In your initial outreach, always highlight your availability to view the property, specifying the days and times that work for you. Also include essential information like your intended move-in date and a brief introduction about yourself. You should begin to sell your qualifications and commitment to renting the space on your initial contact. That's what makes these emails stand out.

2. **Send a quick text.**

   If the ad provides a mobile number, texting is a convenient option. Catering to different communication preferences increases your likelihood of receiving a prompt response.

The more personalized and organized your approach, the more likely you are to secure a viewing appointment promptly.

Meeting leasing agents and property managers

Establish a well-organized touring schedule that accounts for potential travel time, parking, and unforeseen delays. Be on time for your meeting with the leasing agent or property manager. Arriving a little earlier than scheduled may provide an opportunity for a one-on-one conversation with them. This personal interaction lets you introduce yourself and express your excitement about the space. In competitive rental markets, where every advantage matters, being among the first to see a property can be a game-changer.

Be proactive about preparing questions before each viewing. Don't hesitate to ask about any aspects you need clarification on, and make sure to take notes during your visit. Engaging in meaningful conversation establishes a positive rapport that can be valuable throughout the application process. Make the most of this interaction by sharing relevant information and engaging in small talk.

Connecting with the leasing agent or property manager leaves a lasting impression. If you decide to proceed with the application, they'll convey this impression to the owner, which can work in your favor during the approval process. If you're confident that the space suits your needs, don't hesitate to express your interest and request the next steps for the application.

TIP

Consider bringing along your application documents or having them well organized for quick email submission after viewing the space. If you decide to apply, you can quickly provide your paperwork, showing your commitment and eagerness to move forward. See Chapter 5 for details about putting together your application.

Another detail that contributes to your first impression on leasing agents and property managers: your attire. Your clothes should reflect professionalism or a neat, casual appearance. Agents and property managers notice even the most minor details, including your presentation.

Making the most of your tours

Property tours should be an enjoyable and enriching experience. They offer you the opportunity to explore your future home, interact with the person leading the tour, and, crucially, gain insights into your preferences and dislikes.

With apartments in particular, walk around the property; walk the halls to listen for sounds. Do you hear music, televisions, conversations? Do you feel like you're in the same space as those sounds, or do they come across as background noise that's easy to tune out? Check as many times as you need to feel comfortable knowing whether the space is quiet enough for you.

Note what you see when you look out the windows. Do any tall buildings block light from hitting the home? Is anything else obscuring the views? In short, can you live with these views every day, or will you want to keep the windows covered rather than stare at that ugly warehouse while you're eating dinner? If you're someone who keeps their blinds closed 24/7, such a view may not matter to you, but otherwise, you may want to look for an option with a different view.

TIP

Sunlight gives refreshing and vitalizing energy. To confirm that your home gets abundant sunlight, use a compass or a compass app to determine the direction of the windows and the exposures. In the Northern Hemisphere

>> A room that faces south receives great sunlight.

>> A room that faces east receives early morning sunlight.

>> A room that faces west mostly receives late afternoon light.

>> A room that faces north receives the lowest amount of direct sunlight.

One of the best ways to remember the spaces is by taking a video. Video allows you the time to review the home alone, the chance to see it as many times as you like, and the ability to share it with your friends and family. Other people often see things you missed or provide a different perspective. They may notice defects or imperfections you need to point out to the agent or property manager.

Limit your viewings to no more than four to five per day to ensure that you remember important features.

Being intentional about the home you see yourself living in helps you choose the right place. If something bothers you on the walk-through, you can bet it'll bother you after you've moved in.

Working with a Rental Agent

Embarking on the journey to find your next home brings a pivotal decision: choosing who (if anyone) will guide you through this process. Deciding to work with a licensed rental agent holds significant advantages:

>> **Neighborhood expertise:** A proficient agent has an intricate understanding of the neighborhood you're considering. They can act as a local expert, empowering you to make informed decisions about where to live.

>> **Network:** When you use the services of a rental agent, you open the door to the benefits of their network of landlords and inventory — access to extensive listings within your budget, prompt notifications about fresh listings hitting the market, and quick access.

>> **Dedication:** Exceptional agents go the extra mile, prioritizing your needs above all else and tirelessly working to secure the space you desire. A rental agent saves you valuable time, freeing you to focus on your career, lifestyle, and everything you value.

They're responsible for identifying the perfect fit, meticulously organizing your application for property managers or owners, and facilitating contact details for utility providers. Your agent should be a reliable resource, ensuring a smooth and efficient rental process.

The following sections give you the scoop on finding and working with a rental agent.

Understanding the role a rental agent plays

A rental agent can simplify and streamline the process of finding your new rental by understanding you and the type of place you like, your budget, and the neighborhood you want.

REMEMBER

When you hire a rental agent, you save valuable time. Your rental agent

>> Negotiates for you to secure the best possible deal (market conditions permitting), including negotiating prices, terms, and needs

>> Arranges property showings for you, showcasing the features and benefits of each property

>> Ensures that the transaction complies with local and state regulations and laws

>> Provides high-level customer service, addressing your concerns and questions immediately

>> Acts as your advocate, guiding you from your search to your lease signing

TIP

If you're collaborating with a rental agent, consider sharing your feedback on the properties you view. This input helps your agent better align options with your preferences.

When you engage the services of a rental agent, you should know you'll pay a broker fee at the lease signing, as I explain in the later section "Knowing about the broker fee."

Finding a qualified rental agent

Many people begin their search by seeking recommendations from friends, family, or colleagues who have had positive experiences with rental agents. These referrals often lead to fruitful partnerships and are among the best leads when you're looking for a rental agent.

Alternatively, you can turn to online resources, such as Yelp, Google Reviews, and real estate websites, where past clients share feedback on their experiences with different agents. Additionally, consider visiting local real estate offices in the neighborhoods you're interested in. In-person meetings with agents allow you to learn about their expertise in the area, their track record with clients similar to you, and their approach to assisting you in finding the perfect home.

Be sure to check LinkedIn, where you may find agents with shared business connections. Many rental agents also maintain a presence on other social media platforms, which can be valuable sources for finding potential leads.

Picking the right agent to work with

Selecting the right agent can significantly impact the success of your home search, so your choice is critical.

REMEMBER

Many considerations matter when choosing your rental agent:

>> **Track record and experience in the local market:** The agent should have completed multiple transactions in the neighborhood and clearly understand its nuances, unique features, and attractions. Assess the agent's familiarity with the particular area you're considering calling home, including knowledge of current market trends, rental values, and neighborhood dynamics.

>> **Negotiation skills:** Your agent should have the skills and marketing intelligence to negotiate for you successfully. Determine the agent's ability to negotiate effectively and ask about their plan for securing the best deal.

>> **Rapport:** Working with a rental agent should feel natural and unforced. Work with an agent you connect with. As you interview the agent, think about your rapport with them. You want to feel comfortable and confident about working with

them. Will they meet your needs? Will you be their priority? Make your expectations clear early on, and make sure you're aligned.

>> **Communication and responsiveness:** Your agent should be able and willing to reply to your emails or texts quickly. They should keep you informed throughout the process and be easy to reach.

>> **Past client satisfaction:** Read their online reviews and testimonials to find out about their past client experiences. These accounts may be a good indicator of your future transaction with the agent.

>> **Real estate license:** Your agent should have an active real estate license. Verify their license status and check any associations they're part of, such as the National Association of Realtors (NAR), the Multiple Listing Service (MLS), and other reputable associations.

>> **Connections:** Ask about their local connections and how they can leverage them for you.

>> **Honesty and transparency:** Choose an agent who's transparent and honest about market conditions, rental values, and potential challenges in finding your rental.

Whomever you choose, carefully review the commission or rental fee agreement, including the terms and duration of your time working together, when the broker fee is due, and how much you pay. See the following section for more details on this fee.

REMEMBER

Choosing the right home and agent go hand in hand. When you consider these essential factors, you can feel confident knowing you've made an informed decision.

Knowing about the broker fee

A *broker fee* is a payment you make to a real estate broker or agent for assisting you with finding and renting a place. When you hire a rental agent, you pay for their expertise, access to listings, industry knowledge, guidance, and connections with landlords and other licensed agents. This fee is typically equivalent to one month's rent or a percentage (usually 12 percent to 15 percent) of the first year's annual rent. You make this payment at the lease signing with a certified check, wire transfer, credit card, or electronic payment to the agent's firm.

Clarify the commission you pay before you start working with your agent.

Not all rental transactions involve a broker fee. In some cities, like New York City, broker fees are more prevalent; in others, they're less common. Some landlords cover this cost themselves, and you may find a *no-fee* rental where the landlord pays the broker.

If you prefer not to pay a broker fee, focus your search on no-fee rentals. Keep in mind, though, that your ideal space may fall outside this category, so be open to paying a broker fee for the right place.

Chapter **5**

Application Time

After searching for a dream rental, you've found one you love. Now, it's application time!

In this chapter, you find out about the documents you need, the possibility of using a guarantor, the fees associated with submitting your application, and how to proceed regardless of whether you get the rental you want.

TIP

The first step in getting to a comfortable space with your landlord requires a well-prepared and precise application with all the required documents and an indication that you can pay the rent on time. My experience discussing applicants with landlords sometimes revolves around the professional presentation of the applications prospective tenants submit. That impression makes a difference and helps you stand out in a positive way.

Gathering Documents for Your Prospective Landlord

The first step in being approved to rent a place and moving into your new home requires demonstrating the ability to pay your rent. The landlord needs to verify and review your identity and income.

Here's a quick rundown of the most important documents you need, with more details in the following sections:

>> **ID:** Most landlords require a driver's license, government-issued photo ID card, passport, or original certified birth certificate. These documents should be original; if you must use copies, they should be legible and clear.

>> **Financial statements:** Be ready to show your recent bank statements and investment accounts to the landlord to verify your income and ability to pay the rent. These documents should list all your liquid assets and show your name and address. In addition, your paychecks should show year-to-date earnings. Landlords like to see the last three checks.

>> **Employment verification letter:** This item should be on your employer's letterhead, be dated and signed, and include a name and contact number.

>> **Credit report:** Your credit report should be the most recent. You're allowed to receive one free report from the three credit bureaus per year.

>> **Tax return:** Your landlord could ask for a copy of your tax return. The tax return should be the most recent year filed and include all the pages for review signed by the preparer.

REMEMBER

Your supporting documentation shows your ability to pay the rent on time but also paints a more general picture of who you are. Look at your documents as the beginning of a relationship with the landlord. Your documents show who you'll be in the relationship, so you want them to make the landlord comfortable accepting you as a tenant.

Breaking down the necessary documents

Your future landlord places a very high value on your documents, so they're worth their weight in gold. They determine the level of risk involved with accepting you as a new tenant. A reliable tenant often reduces the landlord's maintenance cost, minimizes wear and tear, and sometimes maintains the outdoor space and property as if it were their own.

The documents you want to include in your rental application are these:

- Cover letter
- Rental application form
- Photo ID (driver's license, passport, government-issued ID) or original certified birth certificate
- Most recent banking statement
- Most recent investment and/or 401(k) statement
- Three recent pay stubs
- Employment verification letter
- Credit report
- Prior year's tax return
- Professional and personal reference letter (optional)

REMEMBER

Although you must verify your income, employment, and savings, the preceding list varies from state to state and even landlord to landlord. Some landlords may require only some of the items from this list. However, your credit report *is* always required from state to state.

The following sections provide some details on basic documents that you may need upfront.

Cover letter

In my experience, approaching the rental process as though you're vying for a coveted job — with a cover letter and resume — leaves a lasting, positive impression. Whether you're looking to rent in a tight competitive market or you just want to ensure that your application is noticed, including a renter cover letter can set you apart from the other potential candidates and increase the odds you sign that lease for your dream home.

REMEMBER

Landlords appreciate a prospective renter who takes the time to share information about themselves, how they found out about the home, and why it's an excellent fit for them. Most landlords gleam with joy knowing how much you'll enjoy living in the space.

Much like the cover letter you'd send to a potential employer, a renter cover letter should highlight your best attributes for the landlord or property management company and show those decision makers you're the best choice among those presented. You want it to showcase your professionalism and responsibility, two qualities landlords prize among tenants.

When I receive a cover letter, I read it to learn more about the client, but I'm also listening for the tone of the letter and how much they're sharing about themselves.

TIP

Be sure to include the balances of your investment, retirement, checking, and savings accounts highlighted in bold in your cover letter. Do the same for your credit score and your salary. The landlord or property manager is paying close attention to these factors, and this approach makes finding that information easier for them.

TIP

Need some templates to help you get writing? Check out the following resources:

>> https://wanbridge.com/educate/
rental-cover-letter-sample-to-rent-a-house/

>> https://rentingitright.ca/
course1/36-resource-cover-letter-template

Your rental application form

Your rental application form is an integral part of your submission. It's where you share personal details. Some application forms request your Social Security number, current address and landlord contact information, previous address and landlord contact information, current employer, salary, and other information to confirm your identity. (*Note:* If this application is for your first-ever rental, you can omit the landlord info.) It sets the tone for your supporting documentation.

If you're currently renting elsewhere, the landlord or property manager will contact any current and previous landlords to verify your tenancy and confirm that you've been a good tenant, so make sure the contact details you provide here are accurate.

For situations where you can't get current contact info for a past landlord, talk to the property manager or landlord about the next steps.

Government-issued identification

Any form of government-issued identification you provide should be current. Landlords typically accept one or more of the following forms of ID:

>> Your current state-issued driver's license

>> A state-issued ID card

>> Your current passport

>> Your birth certificate

Providing a variety of financial statements

You convey your financial picture to the landlord through your bank statements, investment statements, and retirement and 401(k) accounts. These documents show the landlord how much you've accumulated in liquid assets that can be available if you lose your job. Knowing that you've demonstrated the ability to save and manage your money gives the landlord additional comfort in approving your application.

Each financial statement should list your name, address, the name of the institution investing the funds (for investments), and the current value of each account.

REMEMBER

More is more in terms of proof of assets, so put your best foot forward.

REMEMBER

Your financial documents should also include copies of your pay stubs. Having the last three available is ideal. The pay stubs show your year-to-date and biweekly earnings as proof of your ability to cover your rent.

Supplying an employment verification letter

How you obtain an employment verification letter depends on the size of your employer. For large companies, the human resources department is your first stop. Your employer should already have a template to verify employment and work history at the company; whatever that looks like, it should have

>> The company name or logo prominently displayed at the top of the form

>> Your name, annual salary or hourly wage, and length of employment

>> A direct phone number and email address to reach a company official to verify this information

REMEMBER

Make sure your employment verification letter contains these essential elements. Not doing so can delay the application process and prevent approval.

If you've been hired with a future start date, your employment verification may be an offer letter stating your name and address, your expected and confirmed salary/wage, your manager and their contact information, and your anticipated start date.

If you work at a small business, your employment verification letter should come from the owner of the business, a manager or operations manager, or someone that handles the payroll and can confirm your employment at the company.

TIP

For self-employed renters, be prepared to show your tax returns, bank statements, and a letter from your accountant stating your projected annual earnings.

Granting permission to pull your credit report

All landlords are required to check or run your credit history. Your credit report details your monthly payments, *revolving debt* (debt you owe from borrowing against a credit card or a line of credit), total debt, and paid-off account payment history. It also shows any landlord and tenant disputes. This information provides the landlord with past payment history or defaults with other landlords.

WARNING

The landlord can't run or even see your credit report without your explicit authorization. You must complete an application with your Social Security number and authorization to use it to run your credit report. The form should clearly state that by reading, signing, and dating the form, you've given the landlord and the credit authorization company permission to access your credit report.

Authorizing access to view your tax returns

Some landlords require proof of prior year income by reviewing your tax returns. For example, if you're applying for an apartment and have consecutive years of employment, you may be required to show your most recent tax return. The landlord wants to verify that your tax returns support the income you've stated on your application and employment verification letter so they can feel more comfortable that you're a low risk for defaulting or breaking your lease.

REMEMBER

In rental markets that are constantly competitive, tax returns are always required. However, if you're on your first job and don't have substantial prior income, you may be able to get by without them. Just be sure you have a substantial and verifiable reason why you don't have a recent tax return.

Finding a Guarantor (If Necessary)

The road to securing your dream rental home can be paved with obstacles. For example, securing a lease can be tough when you're a first-time renter with no credit or rental history. Other road-blocks include low or less-favorable credit scores or incomes. In these cases, a guarantor can be the right solution.

REMEMBER

A *guarantor,* by definition, is "a person or thing that gives or acts as a guarantee." In a rental context, a guarantor agrees to step in whenever you're not able to pay your rent. Know that signing a lease with a guarantor means that both of you agree to the lease requirements.

Ideally, your guarantor should be someone you trust, like a family member or a close friend. In many scenarios, I have represented tenants with guarantors; they're mostly parents who act as guarantors for their newly graduated children during their first renting experiences.

TIP

In the unlikely event you don't have a family member or friend as a guarantor, you may want to consider a lease guaranty program such as Insurent (www.insurent.com), which I discuss later in this chapter.

The following sections provide more information on finding and working with a guarantor.

Understanding the importance of a guarantor

Why even consider hiring a guarantor? Guarantors support your rental application by covering the gaps or missing pieces required to strengthen your application. They provide your lease with an additional person with verifiable income, a strong credit rating, and liquid assets that the landlord can rely on in the event you run into an issue.

TIP

Regardless of whether you technically need a guarantor to qualify, having a very qualified one can only strengthen your application.

Using a guarantor in certain situations

A landlord may ask for a guarantor in many situations, and those may vary depending on your location, financial situation, or credit history.

Here are some scenarios that may require you to use a guarantor:

>> You're a non-U.S. resident or international student (for example, you have no credit/FICO score, although some landlords may accept your international credit history).

>> You have a low credit score.

>> Your employment history is unstable.

>> You have a low income.

>> Your credit report shows a bankruptcy.

TIP

Before submitting your application, order a credit report and check it for any red flags that may cause your potential landlord to insist on a guarantor. If you see any, proactively line up that guarantor. When the landlord inevitably runs a background check, they'll be able to see criminal records, unfavorable past tenant history, eviction history, your credit score, bankruptcies, and more, so knowing what's on there before they get to it gives you a head start on alleviating those concerns. You get one chance to impress your future landlord.

Making sure your guarantor is qualified

The guarantor pays your rent if you lose your job or have issues coming up with the rent on time, so after selecting your guarantor, the next step is to ensure that they're qualified. They should have solid financials and show strong liquid assets. In some states, your guarantor must make 80 times the rent or double the income required to qualify for the rental.

REMEMBER

The application process you go through is the same for your guarantor, including the documentation (as I describe earlier in this chapter). Time is of the essence when applying for apartments in competitive markets, so make sure that you let your guarantor know promptly which documents they need to gather and that they stay on the ball in providing them.

Working with a lease guaranty program if necessary

If you don't meet the requirements for leasing without a guarantor (see the earlier section "Using a guarantor in certain situations") *and* you don't have a strong network of potential guarantors, you may find yourself with few options.

In these cases, a lease guaranty program such as Insurent (www.insurent.com) or TheGuarantors (www.theguarantors.com/)

guarantees the rent on your behalf. Of course, you pay for the service, and you have to go through the company's application and approval process. But in the long run, using this service can make getting approval a whole lot easier.

Submitting Your Application Pieces in a Professional Order

Congratulations! You're ready to submit your application and move one step closer to moving into your dream rental home.

Renting a place can be a stressful process. Pat yourself on the back for your dedication to the process and for getting this far.

REMEMBER A professional application is all part of the approval process. I can't tell you how often I receive applications that are not put together well. Having your documents in order and all the lines filled in and legible often means that your application gets reviewed first.

TIP Being intentional with the final touches on your application is a winning formula. Here's the order of documents I recommend (find out more about these documents earlier in this chapter):

1. A cover letter that grabs the landlord's attention

2. The application form, where you state your name, address, employer, date of birth, and other personal information

3. Your employment verification letter

4. Your credit report, current landlord reference letter (if applicable), and pay stubs

5. Your bank statements, investment statements, tax return, and identification

I like this order because it starts with personal details about your life, how you got here, and your fondness for the home. Then it goes on to verify your salary, credit rating, and cash savings. It positions your application for success and shows who you are; that you can pay on time, save, and invest; and that you have a good rapport with any current landlord.

Bracing for the First Wave of Payments

Moving into your dream home can add up expense-wise. During your initial visit to the property, make sure that you ask about all the fees associated with a potential move-in, including those attached to filing the application. Allocating funds for such fees in advance is vital to your successful move. Most funds are due at the time your application is approved.

The following sections cover common fees with rental applications.

Paying a one-time application fee

REMEMBER

As the name suggests, a *rental application fee* is a one-time fee prospective renters pay to apply for an apartment or rental house. This money generally covers the cost of screening the tenant, including credit checks and background checks.

Most landlords charge this fee, although the exact price can vary from state to state. Rental application fees usually cost between $20 and $100 per person. If you're applying for a unit in a cooperative or a condominium, they can be a lot higher. (Co-ops and condos are building types I cover in Chapter 3.)

TIP

Depending on your state, landlords may not be allowed to charge an application fee higher than the cost of a background and credit check, so look at your local laws regarding rental application fees.

To pay the application fee, the landlord or property manager may use an online platform or allow you to pay via cash, certified check, credit card, or wire transfer.

Shelling out a fee to your broker

In Chapter 4, I explain why working with a rental agent can be one of the best decisions you make during your rental process. Among other benefits, a passionate and knowledgeable rental agent is an expert on the neighborhood, the inventory, and your profile and has access to listings and landlords (not to mention relationships with those landlords).

REMEMBER

However, working with an agent isn't free. The *broker fee* can be one month's rent or a percentage of the yearly rent (around 10 to 15 percent in some states). Be sure to discuss your agent's fee with them early on in the process so you're crystal clear about how much it is, when it's due (when you're renting a condo or co-op, it's due when the application is submitted), and what payment methods they accept.

For some buildings the broker fee is waived, creating a *no-fee apartment.* The landlord pays the agent.

TECHNICAL
STUFF

Handling move-in fees

Some buildings — often those with a lot of apartments — require a one-time *move-in fee.* This fee helps cover some expenses that come with managing the rental property, such as repairs, maintenance staff, or changing the locks on the doors.

Move-in fees range from 20 percent to 50 percent of one month's rent, depending on the state. Some states restrict how much landlords can charge in move-in fees, so refer to your local state law or real estate agent to ensure that a landlord isn't overcharging.

A move-in fee isn't like a security deposit. Your *security deposit* is returned to you if your apartment is in good condition with no excessive wear and tear when you move out. The move-in fee, however, may or may not be nonrefundable, depending on the type of building and the laws in your state.

REMEMBER

Getting the Verdict of the Landlord

So you've applied for your dream rental home, and the news is in. In the following sections, find out what happens next whether you're approved or denied for a rental.

Good news: You're approved!

"Congratulations! Your application is approved!"

Those two sentences are what I use to tell prospective renters they're approved and ready to move into their new homes. The usual response is filled with joy, excitement, and pure happiness.

For me, too, not just the client. Providing a valuable service that helps you achieve the desired results is a pleasure and honor for me. Witnessing others' enjoyment in their success is something I treasure. Understanding that someone will create lasting memories and get the opportunity to do amazing things because of my

TECHNICAL
STUFF

assistance connecting them to a space that allows them to be their best is quite a feeling.

So often, people overlook how the right home can benefit their lives. The right home allows you to recharge, regroup, reflect, and design your desired life. It truly is your sanctuary. Make sure that you're intentional about experiencing your joy and happiness in finding a new home.

Once you're approved, your next steps are to sign the lease, pick up your keys, and arrange the moving process. See Chapters 6 and 7 for full details.

Bad news: The search for a space continues

The process of finding your new home is emotional. You fall in love with a space as you're taking it all in for the first time, thinking, "This is the one for me." It just feels right. Nothing beats closing your eyes and seeing yourself spending time in your new living room or pulling into your driveway. That warm feeling you get when you visualize these moments makes you fall head over heels for the space — only to be beaten out by another applicant that submitted their application before you.

The feeling of almost — but not quite — having something that resonated with you so quickly hurts. But know a similar home is waiting in the wings for you. I refer to these moments as "the highs and lows of real estate." Picking up your heart, putting it back in your chest, and moving forward with your search again is the best way to move on quickly from the pain of missing out.

I have consoled clients who have experienced this feeling, and I always say, "Don't sweat it. Your new home is on the way." Take it in stride, try to stay positive, and understand that that place wasn't meant for you. The next one is.

Keep looking with the guidance of Chapter 4 and submitting applications with the help of this chapter.

Chapter **6**

Signing the Lease

S o you've done your research, toured a bunch of buildings, and submitted an application to rent a space you love. Good news: You've been approved! Now it's time to make things official.

In this chapter, I discuss the keys elements of your lease. You discover what a lease rider is and what types of details the rider should include. I also cover signing your lease and making sure both parties understand each other's expectations as well as all the payments you need to make upfront and during the term of your lease.

TIP

To check out some examples of leases, riders, and the like, visit the following:

» www.blumberg.com/forms/ lease-residential-commercial/

» www.uslegalforms.com/

Acknowledging That Your Lease Is a Legal Document

REMEMBER

A lease *agreement* is a legal, binding contract between the renter and the landlord, and the court will use it as such if any legal proceedings arise between the two parties. It clarifies responsibilities and terms during the period of the lease (usually 12 months but sometimes 24 or 36). A landlord can enforce the lease against all the tenants responsible for it, so everyone involved needs to understand what their responsibilities are under the lease's terms.

TIP

Because a lease is a legal document, you can expect to see some legal jargon in it. Keep an eye out for the following terms:

>> **Lessee:** A *lessee* or *tenant* is a person who rents property from a landlord (otherwise known as a lessor). The lessee is required to fulfill the terms of the agreement during the term of the lease agreement.

>> **Lessor:** The *lessor* is the person or legal entity who grants a lease to the lessee. The lessor is the owner of the property in the lease agreement.

In the following sections, I go over a lease's key elements, the basics of a lease rider, and whether you should have an attorney review your lease.

Reviewing key elements in your lease

Your lease should clearly state the responsibilities of both the landlord and the tenant. Yes, you're responsible for many important lease elements, such as paying the all-important monthly rent. But what about the maintenance of the residence? Who supplies the heat and hot water for the property? Are you required to make repairs?

REMEMBER

These major items are included in most leases. Here are the important terms that your lease should have:

>> The landlord's first and last name (or name of the entity if the property is owned by an entity).

>> The tenant's first and last name. (Any occupants not listed on the lease should be added as occupants.) Make sure your name is spelled correctly!

>> The address of the property; make sure it's correct.

>> The yearly rent total.

>> The monthly rent.

>> When the rent is due.

>> The security deposit.

>> Deposits and fees (including the fee for late rent, a pet deposit, and the like).

>> The lease start and end dates.

>> The utilities included in the rent.

>> The utilities you pay for separately from rent.

>> Whether the landlord allows pets. If pets are okay, the lease should indicate the type of pet(s) that may live in the property. Otherwise, the lease should state that pets aren't allowed. (*Note:* This info may appear in a rider rather than the lease itself; see the next section for more on that document.)

>> The rights and responsibilities of the landlord and tenant. Examples include the tenant having a right to quiet enjoyment of their home (meaning the tenant is allowed to use the property without disturbance) and the landlord having the right to determine the length of the lease (meaning the landlord can determine if they want to offer a 12-, 24-, or 36-month lease).

>> Adjustments or alterations and repairs to the property that the landlord is responsible for.

>> The condition of the residence at lease signing or before you move in.

>> An inspection of the property prior to the lease signing.

>> The tenant's right to peaceful living (that is, that the landlord can't just drop by to check up on things all the time).

>> How to report repairs in a timely manner to the landlord.

>> The right of the landlord/property manager and service people access to the property with prior or advance notice.

>> Restrictions on subletting the space and the use of it as a short-term rental (such as an Airbnb).

>> Restrictions on illegal activities.

REMEMBER

Make sure you read and understand every vital detail of your lease. Signing your lease is like the beginning of a relationship. Ensure that you know your responsibilities and that you and your landlord understand each other's expectations. You're getting to know each other and want to set the ground rules for the expectations.

Putting together a lease rider

The *lease rider* is a very important document that includes additional details that aren't in the lease. The rider indicates specific conditions that vary from the printed terms of the lease document.

For example, if the lease doesn't include an item about the size of pets permitted, the landlord allows all pets unless a lease rider states the weight and height of pets in the building. Another example: backyard maintenance. If the lease doesn't mention this item, the landlord can insert both parties' responsibilities for the care and upkeep of the backyard with a rider.

The landlord is responsible for drafting the lease and the rider. The landlord sends the lease and the rider to the tenant for review and signature. If the tenant has any questions or suggested edits to the rider, they can request it during the review period. The landlord may or may not accept the request to make any edits. The rider is signed at the same time the lease is signed. Some leases don't include riders because they cover all the needed points in the lease.

REMEMBER

A lease rider should be typed and attached to the original lease agreement. Therefore, adding any terms not included in the lease on the rider is essential. A valid rider should be signed and dated by the landlord and the tenant. I can't overstate this: Make sure any important items or responsibilities both parties have agreed on that aren't included in the lease are added to the lease rider.

Hiring an attorney to review your lease

If you're someone who likes to calculate your risk or requires a deep and clear understanding of every line item on your lease, consider hiring an attorney to review it. The attorney will let you know about any language in the lease that you'd be better off asking your landlord to reconsider, protect your interests, and act for you. Having an attorney look the lease over gives you security in knowing what you're signing up for and prepares you for any worst-case scenarios by informing you of your rights.

Ultimately, however, the landlord must agree to change or edit any lease terms your attorney flags, and you have no guarantee they'll do so. Still, knowing your rights before you sign the lease is ideal.

WARNING

Hiring an attorney can be a red flag for landlords and property managers. They may perceive you as a problem or a tenant that creates an issue on every minor thing. So if you're the kind of person who ultimately requires legal advice for most items, go ahead and consult an attorney. Just be aware that having the attorney contact the landlord may result in your not getting the place.

It's Official! Knowing What to Expect When You Sign Your Lease

Congratulations; you did it! The lease signing day is here. You made it this far; now you're ready for the next steps:

>> **Verify the correct method of payment.** Find the preferred payment method from the landlord, property manager, or real estate agent as soon as you're approved for the lease. Before the COVID-19 pandemic, certified checks were most people's choice because most lease signings were in person. If your lease signing is virtual, most landlords accept the financial app Zelle, wire transfer, or credit card payment.

>> **Get the correct spelling of the landlord's or entity's name.** Make sure you double-check the spelling of the landlord's first and last name. I've encountered many instances where a name's spelling needs to be corrected, causing a delay in the signing or the deposit of funds.

>> **Reconfirm the total amount payable to the landlord.** Remember, if you move in on the first of the month, the first month's rent, along with your security deposit, is payable at lease signing. Find out more about the payments due at the lease signing later in this chapter.

After you finalize the payment details, you're ready to get signing. An in-person lease signing can occur in a few places: in the rental itself, or in the property manager's or real estate agent's office. Ideally, the rental is the best place to conduct the signing.

You can expect the landlord or the property manager and the agent to be present. This could be your first time meeting the landlord in person, so the lease signing is an excellent time to ask questions about rent payments, utilities, anything related to your move-in, and anything you are unsure about.

Inspect the apartment to ensure that any issues you brought up during your initial visit have been corrected. Review your lease for accuracy regarding the spelling of your name, the rent amount, the security deposit amount, and the lease start and end dates. Lastly, if you requested any additions to the lease or changes to any terms, now is the time to confirm the changes.

Three leases should be available for your signature. The agent keeps a copy, the landlord keeps one, and you keep an original signed copy, too.

Making Payments

You're officially a renter! Now you have to pay up. You can expect to make two types of payments to your landlord in your new life as a renter: fees at the time you sign your lease and your monthly rent payment. Get the scoop about both types in the following sections.

Knowing what you pay at the lease signing

Most lease signings require the first month's rent, a security deposit, a broker fee (if you hired a rental agent; find out more about this fee in Chapter 4), and move-in fees. Assuming you don't have to pay a move-in fee, the most important check is the first month's rent and security deposit. Find out more about these payments in the following sections, along with a word about paying the last month's rent.

Security deposit

Your *security deposit* is usually one month's rent (in some states, it's one and a half months). It's designed to cover any excessive wear and tear or significant property damage after you move out; your landlord deducts from it or keeps the entire amount if needed. So if you want your entire security deposit returned, ensure that you take care of the place.

WARNING

Ask your landlord at the lease signing what they regard as excessive wear and tear. Always alert your landlord immediately for any repairs, leaks, and so on. Before signing the lease, inspect the residence for any damages, and make sure your appliances and light bulbs are working.

First month's rent

You pay your first month's rent before you move in to cover your first month of living in your home. You usually make this payment by certified check, wire transfer, Zelle, money order, or credit card. Digital platforms like PayPal and Venmo may also be acceptable.

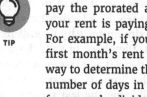

TIP

If you move in during the middle of the month, you should only pay the prorated amount for the first month's rent. *Prorating* your rent is paying for the days you'll have lived in the home. For example, if you move into your new place on April 15, your first month's rent is prorated for only 15 days of use. A simple way to determine the prorated amount is to divide the rent by the number of days in the month. If your rent is $3,000 per month, for example, divide $3,000 by 30 for a total of $100. You pay $100 daily to live in your rental. Then to figure out the prorated rent amount, multiply $100 by 15 days for a total of $1,500. Your first month's rent due at lease signing is $1,500.

Last month's rent

Some states allow the landlord to request that you pay the rent for the final month of your lease in advance. I've seen this approach used for a few reasons. Some tenants use their security deposit as the last month's rent payment (that is, they simply skip paying rent for the final month because they know the landlord has that amount in hand thanks to their security deposit). So to circumvent this situation, the landlord requires first month's rent, last month's rent, *and* the security deposit at lease signing.

Paying the last month's rent in advance along with the security deposit and broker fee is a major financial commitment, so this method ensures that the most financially qualified tenant takes the property and helps remove most of the tenants who may lease the space.

TIP

Asking your rental agent to look only for places that allow the first month's rent and security deposit at the lease signing is a good practice in your home search. This approach ensures that you're only viewing spaces you can afford.

If you're able to pay the last month in advance, your landlord can apply these funds only to the monthly rental dues, not to repairing wear and tear beyond your security deposit. If your lease agreement dictates that the last month's rent is due at the lease signing, and you pay accordingly, you won't owe any rent at the end of the lease term. Additionally, if you renew your lease for another term, this payment typically carries over into the new term. It then applies to the final month when you're ready to move out.

WARNING

Sometimes landlords believe they can charge a new tenant the first month's rent, a security deposit up to the maximum amount, and the last month's rent in *all* scenarios. However, many states consider last month's rent collection as part of the security deposit related to collection limits. In other words, a landlord can't collect the first month's rent, the maximum security deposit limit, and the last month's rent. Instead, they have to split the security deposit maximum between the deposit and last month's rent. Check with your rental agent or the property manager to confirm whether your state allows collecting the last month's rent in advance.

Paying rent every month by check or electronically

Make sure you receive all the rent payment details in advance. The parameters I lay out in the earlier section "It's Official! Knowing What to Expect When You Sign Your Lease" apply here, too: Double-check the correct spelling of the landlord's first and last name, the account details, and the acceptable payment methods for accuracy. Most landlords allow personal checks after your initial payment.

Setting up electronic debit or ACH payments is a simple and effective way to guarantee that you make your payments on time. This method safely lets you automatically deduct the rent from your account on rent day. In addition, it removes the hassle of remembering to write and mail a check.

On-time payments are very important. Paying on time — as well as being a good tenant, being mindful of your neighbors, and being professional with your property managers — makes for a happy and successful stay. Landlords offer lease renewals based in huge part on how often you make timely payments. If you love your new home and community, make sure your payments are on time so you can stay in the space you love.

Taking action when you can't pay the rent

Facing the inability to pay your rent can be scary and stressful. I understand it's a position you never want to find yourself in. However, you can take steps to prevent the situation from getting worse.

The most important step is to notify your landlord immediately when you realize you can't pay the rent or will be late. Communicating in advance is especially crucial if you've been a responsible tenant up until this point.

Most landlords are understanding and willing to work with tenants under challenging situations. Letting your landlord know in advance allows them to help you. They may offer a payment plan or another solution to help you navigate your financial challenges. Being in good standing with your landlord beforehand can greatly increase the likelihood of receiving their support during difficult times. Their assistance can give you the time to raise funds or catch up on your payments.

Another option is seeking emergency rental assistance. Government and private organizations exist that help tenants in situations like this. From the Salvation Army to the U.S. Department of Housing and Urban Development, such groups offer one-time help to those who can't cover their monthly rent. You have many choices, no matter how much assistance you may need. Visit www.consumerfinance.gov/housing/housing-insecurity/

help-for-renters/get-help-paying-rent-and-bills/ or dial 211 to find resources. Another resource is https://home.treasury.gov/policy-issues/coronavirus/assistance-for-American-families-and-workers/emergency-rental-assistance-program. You should check out this step if you can't receive help from your landlord.

You can also consider a loan to cover your monthly rent if nothing else works. You can borrow money from a friend or family member and offer to pay them back later. You can also go to a bank if you can't find anyone close to give you money. I suggest a bank loan as your last option. Borrowing money can dig you into an even deeper financial hole than you were in before, so consider whether it's the best choice in this scenario.

WARNING

One of the first things that can happen if you can't pay rent is that your landlord may try to evict you if you haven't informed them of the situation and worked out a payment plan or solution. Failure to pay rent is a breach of the lease. From that moment forward, you need to find money to cover the rent or move out of the property as soon as possible.

REMEMBER

So, if you find yourself in this situation, please let your landlord know and work out a payment plan to ensure that you catch up on your rent. Most landlords don't want to go through an eviction process. If you've been a great tenant and have a solid track record, they want to keep you in the space and set up an arrangement to get caught up.

3

Settling In to Your New Home

Chapter 7

Congratulations! You're Moving In

Wow, you did it! Moving into a new home is an accomplishment. It's a fresh start and a new beginning.

With so much competition and so many rental homes to view, moving requires a step-by-step plan and a commitment to seeing it through. The move-in is no different.

In this chapter, I discuss the joys of receiving the keys to your new rental and what to check for in your final inspection. I also explain the process of vetting and hiring a professional moving company and give you plenty of packing pointers.

First Things First: Getting the Keys and Taking Another Tour

Getting the keys.

These words are magic to my ears (and probably yours, too)! They mean you've done everything you needed in the search and application process, and now you can move into your dream rental home.

You can save time by asking ahead whether you'll get two sets of keys and whether the landlord has already checked them to make sure they have a good cut. The ideal scenario is that your landlord says yes and makes two copies available for you.

TIP

If that doesn't happen, no problem. Head over to your neighborhood locksmith or hardware store and make a copy of the single set of keys you do get. (And if you get keys that aren't a good cut, contact your landlord or property manager to get a new set cut.)

After receiving your keys, go to the rental for a second or third inspection. (You'd have already done the earlier inspection[s] while viewing the space initially and just before signing your lease). Flush the toilet(s), run the dishwasher, turn on the stove, run the kitchen sink, check the paint for large cracks, check the heating and cooling, ensure that the light bulbs work; you get the point.

Now is the time — just before you move in — to get those items repaired. If you need anything fixed, an email, call, or text to the landlord or property manager should be your next step.

Hiring Movers with Minimum Hassle

If you plan to use a moving company, contracting a qualified and professional one is essential to your move. Choosing the right moving company can shorten your move day.

TIP

Hiring a good moving company is one of the most important decisions you can make during your move. Of course, you're likely more than capable of handling the packing and moving, but that's a lot of sorting, organizing, and lifting. Movers can pack your things, lift and carry heavy pieces of furniture, and just generally remove some of the tasks on your move-day to-do list.

The following sections have all the necessary details on movers.

Knowing what movers can (and can't) do for you

REMEMBER

Professional movers can handle most of the tasks associated with moving your personal items. Here's what you can expect a professional mover to do for you:

>> Supply packing materials, boxes, and tape.

>> Pack your things in such a way that nothing gets broken in transit to your new home.

>> Disassemble furniture such as wardrobes, tables, or anything else designed to be taken apart and reassembled.

>> Load and unload your items onto/off of the truck for damage-free transportation.

>> Unpack the boxes if you want them to.

Note: Although you may want to handle most of the unpacking, keep in mind that anything the movers pack they'll also unpack if that's part of your contract.

You also should discuss in advance whether the movers will reassemble furniture that they took apart.

>> Remove any empty boxes and leftover packing materials.

WARNING

As you research moving companies, you should call ahead to get a list of restricted items each company *doesn't* move. Here are a few examples of common no-nos:

>> **Flammable materials:** This category includes most garage items, such as gasoline, fireworks, pesticides, and paint thinner. Ammonia, nail polish, and nail polish remover are restricted, as are scuba tanks, darkroom chemicals, and batteries (not counting small household batteries).

>> **Food:** Depending on the distance of your move, movers may not take food items. Unless it's a same-day move across

town, anything frozen or refrigerated is off the table to prevent the food from spoiling.

Open food containers are also a no-go because of the risk of attracting pests or spilling.

>> **Personal items susceptible to theft:** Some movers may also prohibit certain items because of the potential for loss or theft.

Double-check that cash, financial and medical records, medicine, and other personal items are included in your hired moving service.

>> **Unwieldly items:** Some movers don't move cumbersome items like treadmills and elliptical machines. If they do, it's often with a fee attached. These items require an extra workforce and related costs.

Researching and asking questions of moving companies

The proper referral goes a long way in a successful move. How many times have you gotten a great tip about a favorite restaurant, bottle of wine, or even mechanic because someone shares a great experience they've recently had? Probably a lot!

When starting this part of your process, contact your friends and family members for their favorable moving company experiences.

Your real estate agent is an excellent source for this information, too. Ask the agent about their clients' experiences with the company and whether it's reliable.

TIP

As you put together your list of companies, do some research on the movers. Check their websites; their social media channels (including comments about service and customer experiences); Google, Reddit, and Yelp reviews; and their overall online presence. Use services like NextDoor for help gathering reviews and referrals, too. Tips left by previous customers are filled with valuable insights. Conduct complete due diligence on the company and own your moving experience.

REMEMBER

When you speak with a moving company representative to discuss your move in full detail, be completely sure that you understand the following:

>> **How much the move will cost:** This question is the most important. Make sure you get your estimate in writing and ask about insurance for your move (I cover insurance in the following section).

>> **Whether the company does long-distance moves (if you need one):** Some don't, and others subcontract these jobs.

>> **What items the movers do and don't move (see the preceding section for more on this topic).**

>> **The company's method of packing.**

>> **How the company protects your valuable items.**

>> **Whether tipping the drivers is customary:** Be ready to pay the tip in cash.

Make sure your contract with your chosen moving company states all the services the movers will perform and all the approved items they'll move.

Be sure you select the insurance for the move, too. You want to be safe and not sorry if anything is damaged.

The following sections provide more details on insurance and cost for short- and long-distance moves.

Checking out the certificate of insurance

An important part of hiring movers is getting the *certificate of insurance* (COI). A COI is a legal document from an insurance company that protects you and the moving company if your move causes any damage in the building.

REMEMBER

First, speak with the landlord or property manager of your new rental about their insurance requirements for your move-in. They should provide a sample document detailing everything they need to be insured and the coverage amounts. This information is essential because without it, you can't send a COI request to your moving company.

The basic elements and information in your COI should include the following:

>> **Landlord/building manager details:**

- The name and contact information of the landlords/ property managers for the rentals you're moving from and to

- The names, email addresses, and phone numbers of the people responsible for your move-out and move-in (one at each location)

>> **Insurance coverage:** Specifies that the movers are insured for that particular building

>> **Building address:** States both the place you're moving out of and the one you're moving into

>> **Coverage details:** Lists the amount the COI covers and how the certificate should be used

>> **The date the form was issued**

>> **Details of the insurance agent or broker that produced/ issued the certification**

>> **Name and address of the person or business covered by the policy**

>> **Policy number along with its effective and expiration dates**

>> **The list of insurers**

>> **The amount of coverage the policy provides**

>> **Description of operations, locations, and vehicles**

>> **Start and end date of the policy**

>> **Signature of the agent, broker, or authorized representative**

REMEMBER

Discuss the COI with your moving company in detail. Ask the company what it needs from the buildings you're moving out of and into to get coverage for your move. These companies complete this process all the time, so ask any and all questions you're not sure about. They're there to guide you through the process and help protect you and your items.

Being clear on what the rate includes

How much your moving company charges depends on the distance of your move and the size and bulk of your items.

The cost of moving in the United States ranges from $800 to $2,500, with the national average at about $1,400. That's for a two-person moving team completing a local move of less than 100 miles. For long-distance moves, the average cost of movers jumps to between $2,200 and $5,700.

Local moves typically cost less than long-distance moves because long-distance moves involve more resources to complete.

The details of your move, such as a full packing service, can also influence how much you pay for movers. Make sure that you're aware of your final price and any potential increases in price.

Figure 7-1 shows some average moving costs.

Home Size	Number of Movers	Number of Hours	Average Moving Cost
Studio/1-bedroom	2	4	$400
2-bedroom	3	6	$900
3-bedroom	4	7	$1,400
4-bedroom	4	9	$1,800
5-bedroom	5	12	$3,000

© John Wiley & Sons

FIGURE 7-1: Average moving costs including different factors.

WARNING

You'll have to pay a deposit to lock in your date, but you shouldn't make your final payment until after your move. A reputable mover shouldn't require you to make the full payment in advance.

Don't underestimate the price tag of a local move. On average, movers charge between $25 and $50 per mover per hour for local moves. So a two-person team working for four hours costs at least $200 to $400 just for labor. That doesn't include other expenses, like transportation fees, materials, and gas.

If you're making an out-of-state move, you need to check on several cost-related issues when hiring a moving company:

WARNING

>> Schedule an in-person estimate and walk-through to discuss in detail the items you're moving and want packed.

Skipping this critical step can leave you with additional charges for items the moving company didn't calculate for your move.

>> Find out whether the company charges a flat fee or an hourly rate.

>> Inquire about any discounts for students, first-time movers, and friends and family.

Scheduling the move

After you've researched moving companies and discussed the details of your move in full (see the preceding sections), you're ready to schedule the move.

Booking early improves the chances of your moving company having availability and offering you a better rate. I believe booking your move a couple of months in advance may be a good idea for some people. During the height of the moving season (spring and summer), some companies' schedules may fill up weeks or even months in advance.

TECHNICAL STUFF

Also, since the start of the COVID-19 pandemic in 2020, more people are moving across the country and filling up schedule spots.

TIP

Consider planning your move between October and April. This period is the off-season for the moving industry. As a result, some moving companies lower their rates during the fall and winter.

So Much Stuff! Packing Your Belongings

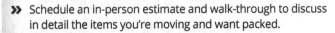

Obsessing over order and organization is the key to a successful pack. Before you pack, I recommend creating a checklist to help you stay organized and ensure that you have the basic items you need.

Start by gathering the supplies you need for packing. The following items should be your go-to essentials as you prepare for your move:

» **Boxes:** For obvious reasons, boxes are the main packing priority. Having multiple sizes for your items makes organizing easier.

» **Tape:** You can never have too much robust, secure tape to seal your boxes. Ensure that you have enough because you don't want to run out and not be able close the top and bottom of your boxes.

» **Pocket knife/scissors:** A sharp knife or scissors to cut the tape and other materials helps make packing easier and more seamless.

» **Permanent marker:** Labeling your boxes is a time saver. It helps you keep track of your items, stay organized, and place them in the correct room in your new home. You don't want to lose track of what was packed in which box. Having to search for important items on a moving day wastes valuable time.

» **Blankets:** You can use blankets for additional padding of mirrors and other breakable items. Be sure you have extras.

If you're bringing in movers (as I explain in the earlier section "Hiring Movers with Minimum Hassle"), check ahead with them about blankets.

» **Bubble wrap and newspaper:** Bubble wrap protects your items from damage and provides a secure way to transport your items. Newspaper can protect glass and other delicate items from scratching or breaking.

Even with bubble wrap and newspaper, be sure to place these items in safe and sturdy places during the move.

» **Handcart/dolly:** Using a handcart or dolly can help with lifting and moving heavy items and boxes and reduce the chance of injury. They also just make your moving life easier.

If you hire movers, speak with your moving company about whether it provides these items. Most moving companies offer them as part of the service, but double-check whether yours adds additional charges for them.

The following sections provide some pointers on getting rid of items that no longer work for you and packing up specific items.

Getting rid of what you don't want or need

The key to moving is deciding what you don't need weeks before your move. Don't wait until your move date to purge your space of unused items. Instead, carve out an hour or two daily to tackle a room or closet. By breaking down your task, you give yourself the time and mental space to comfortably determine what you're keeping and what you no longer have any use for. Doing all this work in a day or two may tempt you to rush and keep items you don't need (or throw away items you later realize you'd find helpful).

Staying organized and ensuring that you're not transporting items you no longer use or need is essential to a clutter-free and organized lifestyle. The following list helps you prepare for the first steps in moving to your new home:

>> **Plan at least two weeks in advance.** Give yourself time. Don't wait until the day before the movers arrive to decide what to pack and what to get rid of.

>> **Have an essentials box for everything you'll need the day you move in, such as a roll of toilet paper, a box cutter, a hammer, and nails.** Label the box in a bright color different from the color on the other boxes and keep it with you while you move so you can get to it right away without digging through all your boxes looking for a necessity.

>> **For every room, bring three boxes: one for stuff to keep, one for stuff to throw away, and one for stuff to donate or sell.** These are separate from your essentials box. Place each item into one of the three boxes as you go through closets and drawers.

>> **Leave the more complicated decisions for last so you don't get frustrated with decluttering.** Eliminating items you never liked is much easier than tossing something with sentimental value, so take those easy wins first to build your momentum for dealing with unused but sentimental gifts.

>> **Donate or sell items in that final box after you've finished digging through every room in your home.** You'll be free of the clutter and make a little bit of cash (or a tax deduction) to help offset your moving costs. That's a win for your efforts; what a great feeling.

Stick to what works best for you. Break down your goal of eliminating unused items one day at a time. Don't try to do it all at once; start your move early by slowly going through your things. You want a lean, organized, and efficient moving experience.

Boxing up items in specific rooms

When figuring out how to pack a bedroom, the following pointers can help keep you organized throughout your moving process:

>> Leave hanging clothes on hangers and place them directly in boxes or moving containers.

>> Keep shoes in their boxes or place them inside a larger box.

>> Store bed linens and pillows in trash bags to keep dust out. Place those bags in labeled boxes.

>> Cover mattresses and furniture with old sheets and blankets.

Dining rooms typically have a high concentration of fragile items — mostly glass and wood — so be extra mindful of those items when packing up your dining room. Be sure to consider the following to ensure that your dining room items stay safe:

>> Use kitchen towels, newspaper, cardboard pieces, and linens to pad boxes and protect plates, glass mugs, and cups.

>> Roll rugs up and secure them with plastic ties or rope.

Kitchen items should be wrapped in protective covering and labeled "Glass/Fragile." Use old newspapers, bubble wrap, or a moving blanket for protection.

Bathroom items should be packed in plastic zip-top bags. Use bubble wrap for protection and a permanent marker to label the bags.

For your books and office materials, start by taping the bottom of each box together; use a good amount of tape so that it's secure.

>> Your books should be placed in an upright position inside the box.

>> Your office supplies should be wrapped together in bubble wrap and labeled.

Chapter **8**

Footing Expenses Beyond Rent

Paying for a rental involves more than just rent. In this chapter, you find out about the utilities in your new home and how to open utility accounts. You also discover renter's insurance along with some tips on how to select the right company for you and why having it is a smart idea, even if your landlord doesn't require it.

Keeping the Utilities On

One cost you need to consider beyond just paying the rent on your new place is utilities. Your utilities keep the rental warm in the winter and cool in the summer. They power appliances like the dishwasher you use every night and the stove you use to cook your favorite plate of pasta.

The following are the most common types of utilities you'll find in your new home:

>> **Electricity:** This utility keeps the lights on — literally! It powers everything in your rental. In addition, some rentals may have electric heat.

>> **Natural gas:** *Natural gas* is a fossil fuel used as an energy source. In rental properties, it often powers heating and cooking. (If you have a gas stove, you use natural gas for cooking.)

>> **Water and sewer:** Without water and sewer, no home is habitable. These two utilities typically come together as a bundle, often provided by one utility company.

>> **Trash and recycling.**

>> **Wi-Fi, cable, streaming services, and phone.**

The following sections show you how to determine which utilities are included in your rent, set up utility accounts, and pay for utilities that are separate from your rent (on time, of course!).

Knowing which utilities the rent includes

You must ask your landlord which utilities (if any) your rent covers and which utilities you pay for separately. As the tenant, you're usually responsible for paying for at least some utilities. The cost can quickly increase, so be sure that you know what you're getting into when signing your lease (see Chapter 6).

REMEMBER

You may find yourself in any of multiple scenarios for who pays for the utilities. The most common are as follows:

>> Your utilities are included in your rent. (You're still paying for them; the landlord just adds to the rent based on their yearly calculations to cover the cost.)

>> The landlord pays for some utilities (perhaps water and sewer). You pay for others (for example, electricity and gas).

>> You pay all utilities separately from the rent payment. In this scenario, you control the utilities, so you're paying only for what you use.

REMEMBER

Before you sign a lease, understanding which utilities are your responsibility is crucial. The lease should clearly state which utilities you pay and which the landlord covers. The following list outlines who commonly pays for what, although arrangements can vary:

>> **Electricity:** In most scenarios, the tenant pays for electricity, but in some cases the landlord pays.

>> **Gas:** If the apartment building or complex has one common boiler, the landlord covers the gas.

If you have your own boiler or furnace and you control the thermostat in your rental, chances are you're paying that bill.

>> **Water and sewer:** The landlord may require the tenant to pay for water and sewer expenses, although this bill can be split between the tenant and the landlord.

In some instances, if you're renting a single-family house, there is a chance you will pay all or a portion of the water and sewer expense. If you're considering renting an entire house, make sure you ask who pays for the water and sewer.

>> **Trash and recycling:** Often, if you live in an apartment building with many units, you use shared garbage and recycling containers.

However, if you're renting a house or similar stand-alone unit, your landlord may hire someone to remove the trash and recycling or be more likely to ask you to cover your trash removal and recycling costs and set up a payment method with the city or a contractor.

>> **Wi-Fi, cable/streaming services, and telephone:** The renter nearly always pays for these utilities. That's because they aren't considered essential elements for living comfortably in your home.

Tip: Contact your mobile carrier about bundling these utilities as an option.

Setting up utility accounts

Your lease tells you which utilities you're responsible for outside of your rent. Then you need to set up utilities accounts for those. Speak with the property manager or landlord about who to contact to set up your account.

Each utility provider has its own set of items it requires to set up an account, but here's a list of common requests:

>> **The address of your new home:** Be sure you include the unit number if you're moving into an apartment or condominium.

>> **Meter number for your new home (for metered utilities such as water and electric):** This item may not be required, but having it handy can help expedite the process.

This number should be visible on the meter itself; your landlord may also have it.

>> **Forms of identification:** A driver's license, Social Security card, or passport are sufficient.

>> **Email address:** Know which email address you want to use for bills and other communications. You may need to be able to access the email while you're setting up your account.

Make sure you contact the utility provider in advance (at least a week should do). You don't want to move into the rental and not have working lights, water, or gas. Plan accordingly when moving to be sure that these utilities remain on when you move in.

Be sure the utility representative is aware of your move-in date. Your service should begin the day you move in.

You should also be prepared to provide a security deposit. Some utility providers require a deposit before setting up service, especially if you have no prior history with them. The deposit amount varies depending on the provider and the type of service. Discuss this issue in detail with the customer service representative.

Lastly, be ready to schedule an appointment to allow a technician to visit the rental if necessary.

Paying for utilities

Utility bills may all come separately, or some may be bundled (like trash and recycling).

Each provider has a billing cycle with different due dates. Some providers bill you each month, while others may bill you every other month or even yearly. Be sure to make on-time payments to avoid any late fees.

Utility companies make scheduling/completing payments and paying your total balance easy. In many cases, you have multiple options you can choose from to make your payments.

The following list helps you understand different bill payment options:

>> **Online bill payment:** You can choose between making one-time payments or setting up recurring automatic payments using your bank or credit union's online web services.

>> **Money order:** No personal banking information appears on the money order.

>> **Credit card:** With a credit card, proving payment is easy if a dispute arises.

   Note: Many providers charge an extra convenience or processing fee for paying with credit cards, so make sure to budget for that amount if applicable.

>> **Cash:** When you use cash, you're not incurring debt.

>> **Check:** You can mail checks, and they're another easy way to prove payment.

TIP

You may want to discuss level billing with utility providers to avoid seasonal increases in your monthly payments. For example, if you have a window or portable air conditioner or a space heater, your electric bill is likely to be higher during the months that see extreme weather. *Level billing* is a payment option designed to provide more consistent and predictable monthly utility bills by averaging the annual energy usage over a set period. Choosing level billing removes the seasonal increases in your monthly utility bills. Be sure to discuss this option with your utility company if you're interested.

You may be able to get an estimate of how much your utilities will cost each month and take out some of the guesswork. To understand the average utility bill for a given property, ask the following people about average utility costs:

>> **Landlord and property manager:** Apartment building landlords and managers nowadays are well informed about the potential utility-related issues new tenants may face. They may be able to provide some insight about your rental's

typical usage. Some have actually incorporated utility costs into the rent price based on the unit size. This way, occupants don't have to worry about the significant utility expenses, such as heating, air conditioning, gas, water, and trash removal.

Flip to the earlier section "Knowing which utilities the rent includes" for more on understanding rent-covered utilities in your lease.

>> **Your utility provider:** Ask the provider of each service for the prior tenant's average use and monthly cost. Keep in mind that their usage and habits may differ from yours, so these numbers may or may not reflect your potential bills.

>> **Your real estate agent:** Your agent should be able to contact the previous tenant to request the prior year's usage and annual cost.

When working with a landlord and previous tenant, I usually ask for these numbers in advance. They happily provide me with estimates in case the new tenant requests them.

The average costs for U.S. households' utilities in recent years are in the nearby sidebar "Money matters: Utility costs in the United States."

MONEY MATTERS: UTILITY COSTS IN THE UNITED STATES

According to the U.S. Energy Information Administration (EIA), in 2021 the average electric bill among U.S. residents was $122 per month. The average bill was lowest in Utah ($82) and highest in Hawaii ($178).

The average U.S. family spends more than $1,000 per year on water costs; the U.S. Environmental Protection Agency indicates that the average water bill is about $83 per month.

The most recent figures available from the American Gas Association puts the average gas bill at $670 per year, or $56 a month, in 2020. But that amount depends a lot on where you live, because the retail price of gas varies from state to state. The cost of gas in Hawaii and Florida, for example, is much higher than in Arkansas and Alaska, according to the EIA. Larger homes and those with gas-powered appliances, like furnaces, water heaters, and stoves, also produce higher gas bills.

Move.org, a moving resource site, found that the average utility costs per month are

- **Electricity:** $117.46
- **Natural gas:** $61.69
- **Water:** $45.44
- **Garbage and recycling:** $25 to $100 (it varies a lot by your location and the size of your trash cans)
- **Broadband internet:** $59.99
- **Streaming services:** $48.25

That comes to $357.83 (plus $75 more if your trash pickup is particularly expensive).

Purchasing Renter's Insurance

The property owner's insurance policy covers the building and any damages to the interior and exterior of the property. The term *renter's insurance* refers to property insurance that protects tenants who live in a rented property.

Renter's insurance covers you and your stuff. Although renter's insurance isn't always a legal requirement, some landlords require their tenants to have coverage before signing a lease and moving in.

The following sections explain the purpose and benefits of renter's insurance as well as how to find and pay for a policy.

Knowing why you need renter's insurance

Regardless of whether you live in an apartment, a single-family home, a co-op, or a condominium (all of which I discuss Chapter 3), insurance companies offer a range of policies designed to protect your personal property against damage, theft, and any unforeseen events that aren't caused by a structural problem with the property. These policies also cover living expenses when someone makes an insurance claim after their unit is damaged.

According to RenterQuotes.com, renter's insurance covers you for the following items (see https://renterquotes.com/Article2.php for more information):

>> **Your personal belongings:** "The policy covers the value of a tenant's possessions. The higher the value, the more expensive the policy is."

>> **Liability:** "If a person is injured in a renter's home or the tenant causes damage to a guest's personal property, the renter's insurance policy will cover the liability of the renter."

>> **Other accommodations:** "If you are not able to return to your rented home after a fire or natural disaster, your renter's insurance will cover the cost of alternative accommodation."

Even if it's not required by law, renter's insurance is a smart choice. Why? Let me count the ways:

>> **Some landlords won't sign a lease unless you show proof of renter's insurance.**

>> **Renter's insurance provides coverage for your personal belongings in case they're damaged, stolen, or destroyed by fire, theft, vandalism, or certain natural disasters.** This coverage can help you replace or repair your belongings, such as furniture, electronics, clothing, appliances, and more.

>> **It provides you with peace of mind knowing that you have financial protection against unforeseen events.** It can give you confidence knowing that you have coverage in many emergencies, which can alleviate stress and worry.

Having renter's insurance is clearly a win-win for you.

Seeing what your lease says about renter's insurance

Your lease is an integral part of renting your home. It outlines your responsibilities and the landlord's responsibilities during your tenancy. If your lease doesn't clearly state the terms and conditions regarding renter's insurance, your *lease rider* (which includes details not in the lease) should. I cover leases and riders in more detail in Chapter 6.

Discuss whether renter's insurance is required during your early visits to the property with your rental agent or the property manager. Before signing your lease, make sure you understand the terminology and requirements of your lease and rider regarding the landlord's expectations about renter's insurance.

Getting referrals and researching renter's insurance

Finding a renter's insurance company should be a smooth process. I always advise renters to start with asking their friends, family, and colleagues for positive experiences they've had with their renter's insurance companies. Getting personal referrals is valuable. They give insight into how the company interacts with its customers and handles claims and your contact's overall satisfaction level with the company.

Also, take advantage of insurance comparison websites. These sites allow you to enter your information once and receive quotes from multiple insurance providers in a side-by-side comparison. This service simplifies comparing coverage options and prices, helping you find the best renter's insurance policy that suits your needs.

TIP

After that, you want to research companies yourself. Forbes Advisor lists its top renter's insurance companies. As of this writing, here are the results; check out www.forbes.com/advisor/renters-insurance/best-renters-insurance for the most up-to-date list:

>> **Best overall:** Allstate (www.allstate.com)

>> **Good for renters with poor credit:** Nationwide (www.nationwide.com)

>> **Great for price:** State Farm (www.statefarm.com)

>> **Best for expanded coverage:** Country Financial (www.countryfinancial.com)

>> **Great for combining with auto insurance:** Westfield (www.
westfieldinsurance.com)

>> **Best for gated communities:** Chubb (www.chubb.com)

>> **Best for families:** American Family (www.amfam.com)

Walking through the insurance buying process

Here's a step-by-step guide to selecting and getting renter's insurance:

1. **To select the best policy for you, start with asking your family and friends for their recommendations for good renter's insurance companies.**

   Specifically ask for recommendations where they've had an exceptional customer service experience.

2. **If Step 1 doesn't provide any good options, research companies that provide positive customer experience reviews along with competitive prices.**

   Be sure to connect with these companies to discuss coverage.

3. **Collect the information you'll need during the sign-up process.**

   This list includes personal details, such as your name, contact information, and date of birth.

   You also need information about the rental property, such as the address, type of dwelling, and any other security features.

4. **Think about the coverage you need for your personal belongings.**

   Take an inventory of your possessions, estimate their value, and consider any high-value items needing additional coverage.

   Also think about liability coverage to protect yourself if someone gets injured in your rental.

5. **Reach out to the insurance companies you identified in Steps 1 and 2 and request quotes for renter's insurance.**

   Provide them with the necessary information you gathered in Step 3 and specify the coverage limits and deductible you prefer.

6. **After you complete your due diligence, compare the quotes and policies and select the renter's insurance policy that best fits your needs and budget.**

7. **Contact the insurance company you want to use, and complete the application form it provides.**

8. **After the carrier approves your application, pay the premium for the policy.**

   You can usually do so monthly or annually, depending on the terms the insurance company offers. (See the next section for details.)

9. **Carefully review the terms and conditions of your policy.**

   Make sure that you clearly understand what your policy covers, what it excludes and limits, and how to file a claim.

REMEMBER

10. **Put your proof of insurance somewhere safe, and provide the landlord with a copy if requested.**

   After you complete the sign-up process and pay the premium, the insurance company provides proof of insurance. This item is typically in the form of an insurance policy document or certificate.

REMEMBER

You now have renter's insurance!

Paying for renter's insurance on a regular schedule

Most renter's insurance providers offer monthly and annual payment options:

>> **Monthly payments:** This approach allows you to spread the cost over smaller, more frequent installments.

>> **Annual payments:** If you prefer to pay upfront and avoid monthly installments, you can pay your entire year's premium in a lump sum. This option sometimes provides cost savings because some insurance companies offer discounts for paying annually.

Whether you go monthly or annual, paying your renter's insurance premium is simple and easy. Several convenient methods are available to ensure your payments arrive on time.

Here are some of the best ways to make your payments:

TIP

>> **Automatic payments:** Automatic electronic funds transfer (EFT) or setting up recurring payments through your bank account save you the time and hassle of remembering to make the payment.

To avoid additional fees for late payment, I suggest signing up for automatic payments.

>> **Online payments:** Most insurance companies have online payment portals on their websites. These interfaces let you make payments securely by using your credit card, debit card, or bank account.

In addition, online payment portals offer convenience and flexibility, allowing you to make payments at any time of day that's convenient for you.

>> **Check or money order:** Some insurance companies still accept traditional payment methods such as checks or money orders. You can mail your payment to the insurance company's designated address if you prefer this method. Ensure sufficient time for the payment to reach the company before the due date.

Chapter **9**

Living with Humans and Other Creatures

Knowing how to get along with others — whether they're roommates, neighbors, or pets — will only enhance your renting experience.

In this chapter, you discover tips and tricks for living in close proximity with others in your rental, whether that's a neighbor, a roommate, or a pet.

Sharing a Wall with Your Neighbors

Living close to neighbors in an apartment building calls for thoughtful consideration. In the following sections, I address how to gracefully handle common situations that affect neighbors in this situation.

REMEMBER

Sharing an apartment wall with your neighbor can be an uneventful experience as long as you're intentional about keeping the noise down and being considerate.

Staying mindful of noise

TIP

Being aware of shared walls and sounds and taking proactive measures can prevent conflicts from arising. By implementing the following tips, you can help mitigate potential disagreements and enjoy a tranquil living experience:

» **Proactively establish a connection and a good rapport with your neighbors.** Initiating conversations and building a solid relationship makes approaching your neighbor easier if you need to discuss noise levels later on. This open line of communication promotes understanding and allows for a more amicable resolution.

» **When determining the layout of a room, consider facing any speakers or TVs toward your living space.** That is, try not to put your neighbor's walls on blast. Being considerate and thoughtful in this way can create a more enjoyable living environment for you and your neighbors.

» **Watch the volume of music, movies, and your voice especially when in rooms adjacent to your neighbors.** This step is so important during late hours.

» **Try soundproofing by strategically placing foam at the back of your furniture, specifically a large bookshelf or wardrobe.** You can minimize the sound waves, creating a quieter and more peaceful atmosphere. This minor adjustment has a significant impact on reducing unwanted noise.

» **Use headphones when enjoying music or watching movies.** This solution is my personal favorite. You can fully immerse yourself in your favorite entertainment while minimizing noise, and your neighbors will thank you!

Being a considerate neighbor

When you genuinely care about your neighbors, people notice, encouraging them to care about you. Maintaining positive relations with other residents in your building is crucial for a happy and stress-free renting life.

A bad relationship with a neighbor can make life very miserable. But when you're mindful and intentional about fostering good energy for others, you unlock a safer neighborhood and a friendlier and more comfortable place to call home.

Here are some key points to being a considerate neighbor:

>> **Introduce yourself when you move in.** A friendly introduction goes a long way. Take a moment to say hello and speak about the area. Asking for helpful information like nearby amenities or favorite restaurants shows your willingness to connect and be a positive presence.

Note: That also goes for longtime residents noticing new faces in the neighborhood. The burden of relationship building isn't just on newcomers, and sharing suggestions on local life is a good way to do your part.

>> **Consider your neighbors' lifestyles and take the time to get to know them.** Understanding their daily routines, like work schedules or family dynamics, can help avoid conflicts. For instance, if you know your neighbor works night shifts, being mindful of keeping noise levels down during their resting hours is considerate.

Along the same lines, sharing information about your lifestyle can assist them in considering your needs.

>> **Practice responsible pet ownership by following the house rules outlined in your lease agreement.** This practice includes cleaning up after your pets, observing leash requirements, and minimizing any noise they may cause. Find out more about living with pets later in this chapter.

>> **Maintain the property's cleanliness and help keep the common areas clean and tidy.** Throw away trash properly, clean up after yourself, and encourage other residents to do the same.

See Chapter 10 for more details on keeping your unit clean and Chapter 12 for guidelines on responsibly using common areas.

>> **If your building offers parking, avoid blocking driveways or tightly spaced spots.** Leave sufficient space for the vehicles behind or in front of you to enter and exit comfortably. Park only in your designated location and ensure that your vehicle doesn't block anyone else's parking area.

Flip to Chapter 12 for more about following parking rules.

>> **Communicate with your neighbors when hosting a party.** Provide advance notice of your event, including the start time and how long you expect it to go on. Share your mobile number in case they need to reach you to address any issues with noise. If you have a friendly relationship with your neighbors, consider inviting them as well.

Be sure to remind your guests about the building house rules, as I explain in Chapter 12.

Dealing with problems created by your neighbors

As a property manager, I can gratefully say that situations with angry or dissatisfied tenants are infrequent among the residents of the building I manage. The majority of our residents are kind, thoughtful, and pleasant individuals.

However, that's not always the case in all buildings. A problematic or difficult neighbor can make things uncomfortable. To ensure that the building maintains a positive and friendly atmosphere, handling these encounters with care, professionalism, and a clear mind helps maintain a peaceful, stress-free living experience.

REMEMBER

Here are some general guidelines for dealing with problems caused by a fellow tenant in an apartment building:

>> **Contact your property manager or landlord.** If you're experiencing challenges with a problematic resident, reaching out to your property manager (if you have one) or the landlord is the best course of action. They have the expertise and experience to handle and resolve these situations effectively.

Involving the property manager also helps maintain separation and distance from the situation, ensuring a more objective approach to finding a solution. A good property manager is always prepared to address and diffuse any potential issues.

You can read more about working with a property manager in Chapter 10.

» **Approach the situation with attentiveness, patience, and awareness.** If you make the decision to confront the problematic tenant yourself, calmly state what they're doing to cause the problem. Be clear and kind when explaining the issue and how it's affecting your living experience. Allow them to respond, and listen intently and compassionately to their reply. Then engage in a productive discussion and work toward finding a solution. Check out the nearby sidebar "My own experience with a noisy neighbor" for a personal example of this approach in action.

Your willingness to come to a resolution while showing concern for them shows that you're on their side. Establishing a connection through active listening and caring responses can transform the relationship and create more positive experiences.

» **Write a note and slide it under their door.** Maybe the thought of discussing the problem face-to-face gives you anxiety. Writing a letter gives you the space and time to be transparent and clear about the problem they're creating and how it's impacting your living experience.

The following sections discuss specific neighbor-created circumstances in more detail.

When your neighbor smokes

Addressing a neighbor who smokes requires a delicate approach to upholding their rights as a tenant while considering the well-being and comfort of the other residents.

According to the American Lung Association, "Secondhand smoke exposure in multi-unit dwellings such as apartments and condominiums is unfortunately both a common problem and also dangerous for you and your family. Exposure to secondhand smoke can lead to serious health problems including lung cancer, heart disease and stroke, and can make asthma worse in adults and children. It is especially dangerous for children as it can result in permanent damage to growing lungs, and cause respiratory illnesses like bronchitis and pneumonia, ear infections and sudden infant death syndrome (SIDS)."

TIP

The American Lung Association offers the following guidance to protect yourself from secondhand smoke exposure in an apartment (see www.lung.org/policy-advocacy/tobacco/smokefree-environments/multi-unit-housing/secondhand-smoke-apartments for full details):

>> **Refer to your lease or building rules to see whether they allow or even address smoking.**

>> **Check whether your community has laws that apply to secondhand smoke in multi-unit housing.**

>> **If you know the neighbor who's smoking and feel comfortable talking to them, see whether you can reach an agreement about when and where they smoke.**

>> **Talk to your primary care physician if secondhand smoke is affecting your health.**

>> **Talk to your property manager or landlord about the secondhand smoke problem.** Keep records of all communications in case you need them, and be calm and polite when you ask about potential solutions.

   If smoking is affecting other neighbors, ask them to talk to the property manager or landlord, too.

>> **Consider other options if absolutely necessary.** If the property manager or landlord can't or won't fix the problem, you may need to look at alternatives such as lawsuits or moving, but those steps should be last resorts.

When your neighbor is loud

Quiet enjoyment (yes, that's an official term) is your right as a tenant to the undisturbed use and enjoyment of your rental unit. This right is implied in all rental leases, even if it's not explicitly stated. Noise complaints are the most common complaint landlords receive from tenants.

REMEMBER

Normal noise is everyday noise in an apartment, like walking or talking. *Excessive noise* is usually reoccurring and not part of "normal" living — like loud music or a dog that doesn't stop barking.

REMEMBER

If you find yourself dealing with a noise situation that consists of a neighbor habitually screaming or arguing, I suggest you contact the landlord or property manager directly, especially if you're uncomfortable approaching the resident about the noise. These situations often require the property manager's expertise to resolve.

However, if you have some intel on who your noisy neighbors are and are comfortable dealing with them directly, contact them about the noise situation. Be sure you approach them in a professional and friendly manner. Describe the days and times you hear the sounds and indicate that you appreciate their help with resolving this situation. (See the nearby sidebar for my own experience with a noisy neighbor.)

Here are my additional tips for dealing with a loud neighbor:

>> **Keep notes of what you hear and the date, time, and length of each occurrence.** Your accurate and precise notes are helpful if you need to escalate the matter.

>> **Start by having a friendly conversation with your neighbor.** Approach them calmly and politely to express your concerns about the noise. They may not be aware of how their activities affect you, so giving them the benefit of the doubt is a nice gesture.

>> **Review your lease or house rules regarding noise-related issues.** This information gives you a foundation for discussing the problem with your neighbor and seeking a solution.

>> **Contact the landlord or property manager if direct communication with your neighbor doesn't work.** Provide them with your detailed breakdown of the noise disruption and of any previous attempts to address the issue. They can enforce noise regulations and can intervene to resolve the situation.

Be intentional about approaching the situation with patience and understanding. Your neighbor may not be aware of the impact of their noise. Use your sound judgment and intuition before deciding on the next steps.

MY OWN EXPERIENCE WITH A NOISY NEIGHBOR

I experienced a situation with neighbors above me who had a loud television. The bass from their surround sound speakers would often create unbearable noise whenever they turned on the television. Any type of show they watched, I could hear every word.

I preferred to try speaking to them directly before contacting the property manager. I'd already met them a couple of times in the building's gym and roof deck; they seemed like easygoing people, so I was comfortable with bringing this up. I made a decision to go to their apartment if I heard the sound again.

Lo and behold, I heard the consistent bass and sound of the news one evening around 8:00 p.m. I took a trip one flight up and rang their doorbell. The husband answered the door and greeted me with a friendly hello. I returned with a warm greeting and complimented him on his surround sound system. I made him aware that I could hear every movie, newscast, and sports program they watched. He looked surprised and immediately apologized for it. He then turned down the sound and said it wouldn't happen again. I continued with small talk and thanked him, and walked away.

I'm happy to say I never heard the noise again. Later that week, he told me he'd moved the bass speaker from the floor to the shelf. I thanked him, and he thanked me for the heads-up again and said to please let him know if I ever heard it going forward.

This encounter was amicable, courteous, and professional. Given what I knew about their temperament, I'd already presumed they'd be kind and warm, so I was prepared for a friendly and understanding meeting.

When you can smell something foul from your neighbor's apartment

In a 2006 *New York Times* article titled "What's That Smell?" Teri Karush Rogers described one pitfall of living with other residents in a building: "Sometimes, vertical living really stinks. Second-hand smells emanating from pets, cooking, cigarettes, renovations, and even garbage can waft up, down, and sideways among apartments (and occasionally town houses), sometimes hanging in one place — most objectionably, one's own — like a stifling August afternoon."

Odors emanating from the apartment next to or below yours can be a major problem. Whether it's harmful cigarette smoke (as I cover earlier in this chapter), pet urine, or cooking aromas such as fishy odors, garlic, or onions, such scents can cause health conditions and an uncomfortable living environment.

How to deal with it can vary. Often you can communicate with your neighbor politely and suggest opening a window or installing ventilation. These remedies can lessen the smells. But other times, speaking with the property manager or landlord is the best solution.

REMEMBER

Overall, dealing with foul odors requires patience and understanding. Maintain a professional and respectful demeanor throughout the process and focus on resolving the issue versus assigning blame. Clear communication, documentation, and a cooperative attitude help ensure a more positive outcome.

Living with a Roommate

One of the first exciting choices you get to make in finding a rental is whether to have a roommate or go solo. It's an important decision that can bring both joy and significant contemplation. Ultimately, I want you to make the decision that enhances your lifestyle and allows you to live your best life.

TIP

Before you decide whether to have a roommate, consider what you truly desire in your living situation. Do you prioritize peace, privacy, and personal recharge time, or do you prefer an active lifestyle with social gatherings, nights out, and fun-filled moments? You'll continue to seek these qualities regardless of whether you have a roommate. Take your time to reflect on what matters most to you in your home environment so that you make your decision from a place of clarity and create a living situation that aligns with your values and allows you to thrive.

REMEMBER

Before signing your lease agreement (see Chapter 6), determine whether your landlord allows roommates at all. Even if you don't plan on getting a roommate right away, asking this question early on helps you understand the landlord's policy for the future.

Some landlords embrace the idea of roommates, while others may have restrictions, especially if you initially lease the apartment as a single occupant.

The following sections cover the steps of finding the right roommate for your rental.

Tracking the pros and cons of having a roommate

You may find a lot of benefits from having a roommate, but those advantages often come with flip sides that are less rosy. In the following sections, I explore the positives and potential challenges of living with a roommate.

Cost savings (but also relying on another's financial responsibility)

Living with a roommate comes with a significant advantage: the opportunity to split the cost of many aspects of living. Take rent and utilities, for example. You may be able to enjoy a more spacious and comfortable place than your budget would've allowed if you lived alone.

Additionally, you and your roommate can share the expenses for furniture, kitchen supplies, and everyday items like groceries and cleaning products, further lightening the financial load and making your space home without spending your entire savings. Make sure you discuss how you'll split or share costs for things like groceries, cleaning supplies, and other jointly owned items.

TIP

Have a plan in writing for how you'll divide any shared furnishings and other joint purchases when you go your separate ways. Discuss ownership and consider a buyout agreement for the expensive items to ensure a smooth transition. Do this especially if your roommate was a friend first; you want to keep it that way.

Although having a roommate can bring cost savings, a roommate who struggles with meeting financial obligations creates difficulties for both of you. Rent and utilities must be paid on time, regardless of individual circumstances. Late or missed payments may lead to added stress and unexpected expenses.

To minimize the risk, thoroughly assess a potential roommate's work history and financial track record. Conduct a thorough screening process, including reference checks from previous landlords, when considering a stranger. These steps can help protect you against financial burdens and maintain a positive credit rating. Find out more about vetting candidates in the later section "Interviewing potential roommates."

Sharing chores (but also dealing with another's habits)

Having a roommate can make cleaning your rental easier and faster. Splitting the chores can lighten the load and even let you avoid doing tasks you dislike the most.

Create a chore chart or some other accountability system. This way, no one feels overwhelmed with all the grunt work, and you can maintain a clean and happy living space together.

Living with a roommate can also lead to double the mess. Dishes may pile up and trash bins may overflow, with roommates sometimes blaming each other, particularly if they have different standards of cleanliness.

If you already know your roommate and they have a messy track record, they'll likely maintain their habits despite their promises or intentions to change.

Built-in companionship (but also constantly having another in your space)

Living with a roommate you enjoy spending time with can lead to fun times and memorable experiences. Whether you're hosting parties at home, exploring the neighborhood together, or just relaxing over takeout, having a reliable companion by your side adds something to look forward to daily.

But the constant companionship may be less exciting if your roommate's idea of fun is different from yours. Even if they're not all-night party animals, some roommates have loud footsteps, talk loudly, and enjoy late-night music. For lower-key renters, that lifestyle makes finding tranquility and downtime difficult. (And vice versa; if you're the wild child, you may find that a more subdued roommate cramps your style.)

REMEMBER

Living with a roommate means sacrificing some of your privacy. With shared living spaces, finding moments of solitude can be challenging. Even if you find an area of sanctuary, such as your bedroom, that may only offer complete seclusion if your roommate respects your boundaries.

Advertising for a roommate

So your lease says you're allowed to have a roommate, and you've decided you want to get one. Great! Now you just have to figure out how to find someone. The following sections break down a couple of avenues you can take toward finding a roommate.

Dedicated services

Finding your ideal roommate can be an easy and hassle-free experience when you have access to the right platforms for searching and advertising. Numerous reliable apps offer streamlined and efficient services, delivering secure information on potential roommates directly to your inbox or through their dedicated apps.

Here I've included a list of my favorite platforms to help you find a qualified roommate:

>> According to Roommates.com (www.roommates.com), the site "makes things fast and convenient. It takes just a couple minutes to fill everything out. Just tell us some basic information and you're on your way. When someone creates a profile, we let them verify their ID, and indicate this on their profile with a badge. This gives you peace of mind that you're talking to a real person. We do the heavy lifting. Our robust algorithm gathers, combines, connects, and delivers results for those who would be a good fit, and puts them all in one place."

>> SpareRoom (www.spareroom.com) has employees to check each ad and ensure that all postings are secure and real. According to the site, "We're all about people. Everyone's idea of the perfect roommate is different, so search based on what's important to you. Every 3 minutes someone finds a roommate on SpareRoom. With the biggest selection of ads, you'll find yours."

>> Roomster (www.roomster.com) has listings in nearly 200 countries and 20 languages. It matches you with possible roommates based on personality factors, keywords, and hobbies. You also can find a roommate based on friend recommendations and questions answered in their profiles. Roomster lets users link their social media accounts, so more information is available to help users discover the right match.

>> Roomaters (https://roomaters.com/) matches room-mates with the help of a personality test. You'll be able to provide information about your interests, hobbies, and other traits (whether you're social or introverted, messy or neat, and so on).

>> Roomiematch (www.roomiematch.com/) says, "We review roommates before our subscribers do. Anyone raising our scam, spam, or scum red flags is immediately ejected before they get in touch with you first. Quickly determine who is worth it with Roommate Behavior Ratings. We also delete anyone that sounds insincere, completely offbase, or just completely insane, BEFORE they'd see any current subscrib-er's profile. In addition to weeding out roommate scammers, our human reviewers screen all new roommate profiles for other scumbags."

Additionally, numerous Facebook groups are dedicated to facil-itating roommate connections. To explore such groups, try searching for terms like "Find roommates [your city]," "Rentals in [your city]," or "Real estate rentals [your city]." These ave-nues can provide excellent opportunities to connect with potential roommates and find the perfect fit for your living arrangement.

You can also list the available room on Facebook Marketplace, providing specific details about the room and your preferred roommate qualities (for example, pet preferences, dietary prefer-ences, preferred sleep schedules).

Personal connections and referrals

Your search for a roommate requires due diligence, and tapping into your network of trusted colleagues, associates, friends, and family is one way to get a head start on finding a good match. Someone within your circle likely needs a room or knows some-one who does.

Consider making a friendly social media post reaching out to your network or their connections to inquire whether anyone is searching for a room. This approach offers the advantage of connecting with candidates who come with personal recommendations.

You can also take advantage of word of mouth's power and utilize your house of worship, work, or school and alumni networks. Post flyers on community bulletin boards or breakroom noticeboards. This strategy can facilitate connections with mutual friends or trusted acquaintances who may also be seeking a roommate.

Interviewing potential roommates

Asking the right questions while interviewing potential roommates is critical to gaining valuable insight into their lifestyle and financial stability. The only way to know whether your potential roommate is the right fit is to dig deep into their habits and who they are.

To help you get started on the right track, here are a few questions to consider:

>> Can you provide references from previous roommates or landlords?

>> What kind of lease term are you interested in (short-term, one-year lease, long-term)?

>> What's your current employment situation and monthly income?

>> Do you have any ongoing financial obligations or debts?

>> How do you typically handle household chores and cleanliness?

>> What are your general habits and preferences regarding noise, guests, and socializing?

>> Do you have any specific lifestyle preferences or practices that may impact our living dynamic?

>> What time do you go to bed every night?

>> Do you have any pets?

>> What are your expectations regarding sharing expenses such as rent, utilities, and groceries?

>> Can you commit to paying bills and rent on time?

>> How do you handle conflicts or disagreements in a shared living space?

REMEMBER

Data is essential. You want to be sure you're making the best decision, so you need to gather as much data as you can get to make an informed and confident choice.

Picking the right roommate

After you've interviewed your potential roommates, asked all the necessary and challenging questions, considered all the facts about each person, and checked and verified their references and financial information, it's time to make a selection.

Start with the intangibles. Do you see yourself getting along quickly with the individual? What do your instincts tell you about their cleanliness? Are they calm and reserved or loud and high-energy? Are they fiscally responsible and trustworthy? Consider what characteristics you're looking for in a roommate. Do they fit the bill?

TIP

Think about getting a second opinion from someone who knows you well, such as a close friend or loved one, and can help guide you with insight.

After you've considered these factors, make your decision confidently, knowing that you've conducted thorough due diligence. Move forward knowing you've made a well-informed choice and feel optimistic about your chosen path.

Getting your new roommate's documentation

Your new roommate should be prepared to submit whatever documentation your landlord or property manager requires. (See Chapter 5 for more information.) The list may vary from landlord to landlord, but the following documentation is pretty standard:

>> Three most recent pay stubs

>> Photo ID

>> Most recent bank statement

>> Most recent investment statements

>> Last year's tax return

>> Employment verification letter

>> Landlord reference letter

>> Current credit report

>> The rental application page

>> A cover letter

Making Accommodations for Fur Babies

First things first: Ensure that your landlord allows pets. Pet-friendly rentals are in high demand but many are available.

But finding a place that accepts your pet is just the tip of the iceberg. You still need to ensure their well-being in the space while respecting the landlord's rules — and your neighbors' peace. Get the scoop in the following sections.

Familiarizing yourself with the pet policy

Carefully review your lease agreement to understand any specific pet rules or restrictions. Look for clauses regarding the breed, size, number of pets allowed, and any fees or pet deposits. (You can read about fees in the following section.)

Most apartment pet policies limit the number of pets to one or two within each unit. Some pet policies may allow cats and dogs but restrict other kinds of pets, like reptiles or birds.

Many rentals enforce breed restrictions to avoid liability and potential damage to the property. For example, typical dog breeds prohibited on rental properties include pit bulls, German shepherds, and Rottweilers.

Some policies may include a weight limit, which can also rule out many breeds of dogs. The thinking is that bigger dogs may pose a risk to the rental and be a bigger noise hazard. Most rentals that restrict dogs by weight usually don't allow any heavier than 40 pounds.

Contact your landlord or property manager with any questions or clarifications on the pet policy.

Paying a pet deposit and monthly fee

A *pet deposit* is a payment, similar to a security deposit, that you make to the landlord to cover any property damage a pet causes. It's typically a requirement, and it's due at lease signing (see Chapter 6). Like with a security deposit, the property manager or landlord must return the pet deposit after the lease ends if they don't find any property-related damages caused by your pet.

A *pet rent* is a monthly pet fee you may pay in addition to your regular rent. Pet rent allows your landlord to cover wear and tear caused by pets, like stained carpets in an apartment building's lobby and other pet-related damages. Some landlords calculate pet rent as 1 percent or 2 percent of the total rent or charge a flat rate based on market area, pet size, or experience with pets on the property. The average pet rent is approximately $10 to $60 per month.

Before signing your lease agreement, confirm any pet deposits and monthly pet fees with your landlord or property manager.

Being a responsible pet owner when you live in a rental

By considering the following tips, you can create a pet-friendly living space that promotes the well-being and happiness of your furry friend while being considerate of your neighbors:

>> **Determine whether the space and layout of your living area can comfortably accommodate your pet's needs.** Consider their size, activity level, and any specific requirements they may have.

>> **Create a safe environment by removing hazards like toxic plants, chemicals, peeling paint, and loose wires.** Install safety gates in areas where you want to restrict access. *Note:* Any such changes that require alterations to the rental may need landlord approval, as I explain in Chapter 13.

>> **Provide toys and furniture for your pet, such as a soft bed (and scratching posts for cats).** Consider a clean and secure location to place their food and water bowls, litter boxes, and outdoor potty areas.

>> **Make time for play sessions, walks, or trips to the park.** Consider their energy levels and provide physical and mental stimulation outlets to prevent boredom and destructive behavior.

>> **Be mindful of noise levels, especially when neighbors live above, next to, or under you.** Ensure that your pet's activities, such as barking or playing, don't disturb other residents. Pet training can help toward a peaceful and quiet living experience for other residents. (I discuss being mindful of noise in your rental earlier in this chapter.)

>> **Maintain a clean living space by regularly cleaning up after your pet.** Establish a routine for grooming, including bathing, brushing, and nail trimming, to keep your pet clean and healthy and minimize their impact on your rental space.

TIP

The American Veterinary Medical Association offers sound advice and tips to ensure you're a responsible pet owner. Owning a pet is a privilege and should result in a mutually beneficial relationship. Visit www.avma.org/resources-tools/pet-owners for details.

Chapter **10**

Drip, Drip: Getting Help When Things Go Wrong

I have the pleasure of working with a few intelligent property managers — the type who are always thinking five steps ahead. They exhibit exceptional people skills, are good listeners, respond to emails promptly, and, most importantly, have an in-depth understanding of the buildings they service. In addition, their interactions with tenants are always productive and pleasant. You want (and hopefully have!) this type of property manager working in your residence, especially when things go awry (as they inevitably do).

In this chapter, I introduce the role of the property manager, explain when you should call the property manager or landlord for help with maintenance (and when you shouldn't), and give you some steps to take in certain repair and pest situations.

Making the Property Manager Your New Best Friend

The *property manager* acts as a liaison between the property owner and the tenants, overseeing the day-to-day operations and ensuring the smooth running of the property. A great property manager is the difference between an exceptional living experience and your worst nightmare.

TIP

Be sure to develop a good rapport with your property manager. Doing so can go a long way toward ensuring that your questions and repair requests are handled quickly and correctly. Keep in mind, too, that your property manager is an extension of the property owner. Being professional and cordial when contacting them can go a long way toward a happy stay and getting things done in your home.

In the following sections, I explain what a property manager does and how to work well with one at the proper times.

Understanding the property manager's role

REMEMBER

In a nutshell, the job of a property manager is to oversee the management and operation of a property on behalf of the owner while ensuring its profitability, keeping the tenants satisfied, and complying with legal obligations. The property manager is very important to the overall wellness of the property and should represent the building and owner in the best light.

The property manager's responsibilities and duties can vary depending on the property type, size, and the agreement between the property owner and the property manager. Property managers handle multiple aspects of tenant management, including

>> Advertising available rentals

>> Qualifying potential tenants

>> Conducting tenant background checks

>> Preparing lease agreements and enforcing lease terms

>> Operating lease renewals or terminations

>> Collecting rent

>> Addressing tenant concerns or issues

Property managers also are responsible for the maintenance and upkeep of the property, such as coordinating repairs, scheduling regular property inspections, and ensuring that the property meets all necessary health and safety standards. They may also hire and supervise maintenance personnel or contractors.

Contacting your property manager at the correct times

As a property manager myself, I want you to know that reaching out to your property manager is essential to properly maintaining the residence. Contacting the property manager ensures that they can schedule and address the necessary issues promptly. (Find out more in the later section "What the landlord or property manager should handle.")

REMEMBER

Not all problems are urgent and require the property manager's attention. The property manager expects most tenants to be able to change a simple light bulb (for example) themselves. Now, if your light bulb is unreachable or requires unscrewing the cover, it requires property manager attention.

Here are some scenarios in which you *should* get in touch with your property manager:

>> **Major maintenance:** Inform your property manager promptly about repair and maintenance issues beyond what a tenant would reasonably be able to tackle. This category includes problems such as (but not limited to) plumbing issues, electrical problems, and heating or cooling defects.

REMEMBER

Contact your property manager immediately in case of emergencies that require urgent attention. I'm talking about burst pipes, gas leaks or the smell of gas, significant structural damage, or fire. The property manager will take the necessary steps to address the emergency and ensure everyone's safety.

>> **Lease-related matters:** Get in touch with your property manager if you have questions or concerns about your lease agreement, rent payments, lease renewal, or anything else

to do with the lease. They'll provide clarification, assist with lease-related paperwork, or address any issues that come up during your tenancy.

>> **Complaints, concerns, or issues regarding the property or other tenants:** Property managers are responsible for addressing tenant concerns and resolving disputes as they arise. (Serious or ongoing disputes, that is; don't bring "Neighbor A never says hello in the hallway"–type drama to your property manager.)

>> **Move-out:** When moving out of your rental unit, you must coordinate with your property manager to schedule the move-out inspection. This step helps document the property's condition and ensures that any potential damages or discrepancies are correctly addressed and your security deposit is returned promptly.

Contact your property manager through their preferred communication method(s), such as phone, email, or an online tenant portal. Make sure to provide detailed information about the issue or concern you're facing to coordinate a quick resolution.

Working well with your property manager

Working effectively with your property manager is essential for maintaining a positive and productive relationship. Here are some tips on how to do just that:

>> **Familiarize yourself with the terms and conditions outlined in your lease agreement.** This document outlines your rights and responsibilities as a tenant and clarifies what you can expect from the property manager. Understanding the lease agreement helps set the foundation for a good working relationship. (See Chapter 6 for more about leases.)

>> **Establish open and transparent lines of communication with your property manager (as I explain in the preceding section).** Communicate any issues or concerns promptly through the correct channels and be polite and respectful.

>> **Adhere to the property rules and regulations the property manager or landlord sets.** Respect the quiet hours, parking rules, and other parameters outlined in your

lease agreement. Being a responsible and considerate tenant helps maintain a happy environment for everyone.

>> **Make sure that you pay your rent on time according to the agreed-upon terms.** Timely rent payments are vital for a positive tenant-manager relationship and can contribute to the overall smooth operation of the property.

>> **Take care of the property and keep it clean and tidy.** Follow proper maintenance practices, promptly report any damages or issues to the property manager, and seek permission before making any alterations or modifications to the property. Treating the property with respect shows your commitment as a responsible tenant.

>> **Be sure to accommodate property inspections and repairs the property manager requests.** Provide access to your unit and cooperate during these processes. Doing so helps ensure that the property remains well maintained and any issues are promptly addressed.

>> **If you decide to move out, follow the move-out procedures outlined in your lease agreement.** Give the property manager proper advance notice. Ensure that you clean and sweep the rental, including the bathroom and kitchen. Return any keys as instructed. Following the lease's procedures creates a smooth transition and potentially leads to the return of your security deposit, if applicable.

REMEMBER

Following these tips can ensure a pleasant living experience and effective communication throughout your tenancy. It may also result in consistent lease renewals. Landlords like to extend lease renewals to great tenants. (Flip to Chapter 11 for more about lease renewals.)

WHAT SHOULD YOU DO WHEN YOUR PROPERTY MANAGER ISN'T GREAT TO WORK WITH?

Being a property manager, I understand the importance of maintaining a professional and friendly attitude. So, if you find yourself in a situation where a property manager does not exhibit a cheerful demeanor or is in a bad mood all the time, you must remember to

(continued)

(continued)

keep your request clear and firm. Always be sure to convey your concerns professionally and persistently. Continue to outline the issues you're facing and the impact on your living experience.

In this situation, using written communication, whether email or text, to document your conversations and requests is the ideal way to communicate. Be sure to be polite but firm in requesting a resolution.

Knowing Who's Responsible for Which Maintenance and Repairs

You need to refer to your lease agreement to determine who is responsible for what in your rental (see Chapter 6). The specific responsibilities can vary depending on the terms of your lease and the state where you live. However, the following sections break down some typical divisions of duties for you and your landlord and/or property manager regarding maintenance and repairs.

REMEMBER

Maintaining the property is a team effort. Work with your landlord and/or property manager to ensure that your rental home is maintained to the highest possible standard.

What you need to maintain in your rental home

REMEMBER

Typically, tenants are responsible for minor maintenance tasks such as changing light bulbs, unclogging drains, and keeping the unit clean. As the tenant, you're also on the hook to promptly report any maintenance or repair issues to the landlord or property management. Here's what you should expect to handle on your own:

>> **Clean the home regularly to keep it neat.** This task includes vacuuming or sweeping the floors, dusting surfaces, cleaning kitchen appliances, and maintaining cleanliness in the bathroom.

>> **Ensure that the plumbing and electrical systems are in good working order.** Check for leaks, clogged or slow

drains, or damaged electrical outlets. Contact the landlord or property management immediately about any issues you discover.

>> **Regularly maintain the heating and cooling systems.**
Speak with the landlord or property manager about routine maintenance and inspections. Doing so helps ensure proper functioning and efficiency.

Two scenarios are likely:

- Upon moving into the property, the landlord will show the tenant how to change the air filter and even supply a few filters free of charge in advance of their move-in.

- The landlord will pay for and replace the air filter when required. If the landlord has a service contract for routine maintenance, replacing the filter is done by the technician, so the tenant doesn't need to worry about it.

>> **Check and test smoke detectors, carbon monoxide detectors, fire extinguishers, and security systems.**
Report any issues or concerns right away to the landlord or property manager.

Quickly report any signs of pest infestation by contacting the landlord or a professional pest control service. I talk more about getting rid of pests later in this chapter.

What the landlord or property manager should handle

REMEMBER

One of the joys of renting is handing over the repair items to the owner or manager of the property. With that said, inform your landlord or property manager immediately about any of the following:

>> Plumbing issues, such as leaky faucets, clogged drains, or backed-up toilets that you can't fix yourself

>> Electrical problems, such as faulty wiring, flickering lights, or issues with electrical outlets

>> Heating and cooling system repairs

>> Any appliance provided by your landlord, such as a refrigerator, stove, oven, dishwasher, or washing machine, that isn't working correctly

>> Structural issues like cracks in walls, damage to the roof, or water leaks (or damage caused by water infiltration, such as mold or mildew growth)

>> Signs of pests (find out more about pest elimination later in this chapter)

>> Safety concerns, such as broken locks, nonfunctioning smoke detectors, or faulty fire extinguishers

>> General maintenance needs, like peeling paint, loose tiles, or damaged flooring

REMEMBER

Landlords should obey local and state laws regarding rental properties, regular inspection (including giving you the proper notice for entering the rental), eviction procedures, and habitable living standards.

WHEN YOUR LANDLORD WON'T MAKE REPAIRS

If the landlord or property manager is not cooperating and responding to your repair request, here are a few actions to take:

• Create a detailed list of the repairs.

• Take photos and video of the repairs.

• Keep copies with dates and times of your emails, texts, calls, and/or other ways you've contacted them with your repair request.

• Write a letter with these repair issues and requests, and send it by certified mail. Certified mail requires the signature of the person it's addressed to. This method ensures that you know the letter was received.

• Contact a reputable landlord and tenant attorney to discuss your rights and the most effective way to remedy your situation.

• Lastly, speak with an attorney about withholding rent until the repairs are made. Some states require that you pay the rent to the court, so before taking this action, ensure that you've sought legal advice. I recommend this action only in extreme cases, such as consecutive months of no heat or hot water in the winter.

Taking Action When Something Breaks Down

When something stops working in your rental, knowing what to do next is almost as important as getting it repaired, as you find out in the following sections.

REMEMBER As I note throughout this chapter, you should report broken appliances; electrical, plumbing, and heating/cooling issues; and other important problems or repairs to the landlord or property manager immediately. Ensure that you have a contact number or email to get in touch with them as soon as possible. The faster you report an issue, the more likely the problems are to be resolved quickly and without further damage.

You have a leak in your ceiling

REMEMBER Most leaks are considered urgent and require immediate attention and repair. Quickly take these steps to prevent further damage and ensure your safety and then contact your landlord or property manager immediately to report the leak:

» **Move any furniture, electrical appliances, or valuable items away from where the water is dripping.** Place buckets or a plastic tarp under the leak to catch the water and prevent it from causing additional damage. Keep it there until the property manager, landlord, or repair person arrives to assess the damage.

» **If the leak is near electrical fixtures or appliances, turn off the power.** If you can do so safely, unplug the appliance from the outlet to avoid the risk of electrical shock.

» **Take photos or videos of the leak and any signs of damage to the ceiling or surrounding areas.**

Your landlord or property manager should arrange for a licensed plumber or contractor to assess the damage and make the necessary repairs.

The stove (or another large appliance) isn't working

Oh, the pain of having a stove that stops working on the day of your dinner party. (What else can go wrong?) Your landlord/

property manager needs to know immediately, so start with notifying them.

If you're comfortable with investigating, start with the electrical panel and the power outlet. Find the breaker switch labeled "stove" and ensure it's in the *on* position. If it's not labeled, then confirm that all the breakers are in the *on* position. You can also just turn every breaker off and then back on. That should restore power to the stove if there are no other electrical issues. If that doesn't solve the problem, check that the stove is plugged into the outlet correctly. Stoves require electricity (and sometimes gas) to operate.

WARNING

Never try to make any repairs to your stove, electrical outlets, dishwasher, or refrigerator. Report them to your property manager or landlord, who can line up a service technician or someone qualified to do the repairs.

A pipe is clogged

When you have a clogged pipe, you can try a couple of tricks to solve the issue. If you're not comfortable with these methods, contact your landlord or property manager right away.

First, determine where the clog is located. Knowing where it is helps you decide on the appropriate method for clearing the blockage:

>> Many times, you can use a plunger and a little force. Ensure that the fixture has enough water in it to cover the plunger's rubber cup, and then create a tight seal by applying pressure and pushing down on the plunger to create suction. After it's sealed, vigorously plunge it up and down many times. The force generated causes the clogged debris to dislodge.

>> Another way you can sometimes unclog pipes is by using natural remedies. For example, baking soda and vinegar can create a fizzy reaction that helps break down certain clogs. The bubbling caused by the vinegar and soda reacting helps loosen the debris in the pipes. Pour a cup of baking soda down the drain, followed by a cup of vinegar. Let it sit for a while and then flush it with hot water.

WARNING

I never recommend chemical drain cleaners because this method can cause damage to the pipes.

The heat or AC goes out

If the heat or air conditioning system goes out in your home, don't fret. You can try a few things before placing a call to your landlord or property manager:

>> **Start with the power.** Is it turned to the *on* position? If system has no power, check the circuit breaker and verify that the relevant breaker isn't tripped. If it is, reset it and see whether that resolves the problem.

>> **See whether the thermostat is the issue.** Ensure that the thermostat is set to the desired temperature and functioning correctly. Make sure that it has power and that the display is working.

**TECHNICAL
STUFF**

>> **For experienced renters only: Check the air filter.** A dirty air filter can obstruct airflow and affect the system's performance. Locate the air filter in your HVAC system and replace it if it appears dirty or clogged.

These are the simple fixes I'm comfortable recommending before you contact the landlord. In most instances, as a new renter your first step should be to call your property manager or landlord. A faulty HVAC system is a job for a professional repair person. Be sure you consult with the professional in all instances.

WARNING

If the lack of heating or cooling poses a safety risk or causes extreme discomfort, especially in extreme weather conditions, consider seeking alternative accommodations or contacting emergency services if necessary.

Encountering and Eliminating Pests

I'm enjoying my favorite episode of *Imposters* when suddenly I catch a quick glimpse of movement from the corner of my eye. Is it a bird? Is it a plane? Is it a ghost? An unwelcome intruder? Nope; it's just a new bug letting me know it's arrived. Don't you love it?

A study published in the journal *PeerJ* indicates that the average U.S. home has roughly 100 different species of bugs, so the chances that you'll encounter some sort of pest issue in your rental are good.

Contact your property manager or landlord immediately if you see any pests in your home. They'll schedule an appointment for an exterminator to assess the pest problem, identify the type of pests and the extent of the infestation, and provide a detailed treatment plan. Follow the instructions the pest control company provides to prepare your home for treatment. This task may include removing clutter, cleaning surfaces, and temporarily relocating your pets or plants.

On the scheduled date, the pest exterminator treats your rental. They may use various methods, like spraying, baiting, or trapping, depending on the nature of the pest problem. Be sure to ask detailed questions about the chemicals they're using and any tips to keep the pests out of the space. To ensure that your place stays pest-free, follow the exterminator's tips.

An exterminator should seal all cracks, so request they seal any openings you know about. After the initial treatment, they may schedule follow-up visits to ensure that the pests are entirely eradicated.

TIP

Note that bugs come into your home to find food: crumbs, pet food — anything they can munch on. Be sure to sweep the kitchen floor and wipe down and clean your kitchen and countertops after every meal. Put fruits, vegetables, and other items in the refrigerator. Keep items such as grains, flour, and nuts in glass or plastic containers. Take your trash out regularly and ask your landlord about installing screen doors and windows.

To prevent pests, such as rodents, insects, or termites, be sure to do the following:

>> Keep the rental clean.

>> Inspect for any cracks or openings where pests can enter.

>> Before getting any work done, discuss it with your landlord or property manager.

>> If you have a rental with an outdoor space, such as a balcony or patio, make sure it's clean and well maintained so it doesn't attract pests. Trim any overgrown plants, remove debris, and report any issues with fences or gates to the landlord/property manager.

IN THIS CHAPTER

» Deciding whether to renew your lease

» Walking through a lease renewal

» Leaving your rental

Chapter **11**
Renewing Your Lease

S o you've been in your rental home for nearly a year, and now you face an important decision: Should you renew your lease, or should you look for a new place?

In this chapter you find out about lease renewals. How do you decide whether to renew or move on? Will your rent increase if you decide to stay? What important actions can you take to ensure that you receive a renewal? I explore these scenarios and other options (including moving) so you understand the process and know what to expect.

Should You Stay or Should You Go?

REMEMBER

Your home is more than a place that provides shelter. It should provide comfort, peace, and the space to be your absolute best. Deciding whether to stay in your rental home or go somewhere new requires careful consideration of several factors.

Here are some actions you can take as you make an informed choice on how to move forward. Note that most lease renewals come 90 to 120 days before the current lease expires, so start thinking about your plans ahead of time:

» **Reflect on your experience in your current apartment or rental house.** Consider factors such as comfort, convenience, and overall satisfaction. Think about proximity to your office, schools, essential services, and recreational activities. Assess how well the space meets your needs and contributes to your quality of life. Are you happy to walk into your home every day? Does it provide you with a feeling of joy and comfort?

» **Think about your future goals and aspirations.** Does staying in your current rental support those plans? Assess whether the rental's location, amenities, and size align with your long-term vision.

Do you envision growth potential? Weigh whether staying in your current place offers personal and professional growth opportunities. Think about the potential for building stronger relationships within the community, accessing new resources, or utilizing nearby amenities that enhance your lifestyle.

» **Evaluate the financial impact of your decision.** Determine whether renewing your lease is financially feasible. Review your budget and whether the rent fits comfortably within your financial means. Consider any potential rent increases and the overall cost of living in your current space. (I talk about increased rent later in this chapter.)

» **Consider the intangible factors that hold value and are important to you.** This list may include sentimental attachment to the space, a sense of belonging in the neighborhood, or a strong connection with the community. These considerations can weigh heavily in your decision-making process.

» **Make a list of the advantages and disadvantages of staying versus moving on.** Consider factors such as proximity to work, social connections, access to amenities, and the potential for a fresh start in a new space. Also think about location, size, layout amenities, and condition.

Stability and familiarity are a couple of key factors to think about. Evaluate the effects of maintaining your established routines, relationships with neighbors, and comfort with your neighborhood. Consider whether these factors contribute positively to your daily life.

>> **Explore new neighborhoods.** If you're contemplating a change, consider the possibilities outside your current rental. Research different neighborhoods, housing options, and the potential for growth and new experiences in a new location.

REMEMBER

This approach isn't a one-size-fits-all solution to whether you should stay or go. It's a personal decision that should consider your unique circumstances and goals. Ultimately, the decision should feel right to you. Trust your intuition and consider what aligns with your values and aspirations. Take the time to listen to your inner voice and make a choice that resonates with your desires for the future.

Staying Put in Your Current Rental Home

So you've decided that you want to remain in your rental home. Great! The following sections go over some considerations for renewing your current lease.

TIP

Before you sign the initial lease, I recommend discussing the potential for renewals and rent increases with your landlord. See Chapter 6 for details on signing your initial lease.

Knowing what to do so you're offered a lease renewal

After you've decided you want to renew your lease, your landlord considers your tenancy during the term and chooses what to do from there. I outline the key elements the landlord or property manager evaluates in this section.

REMEMBER

Your best bet is to communicate directly with your landlord or property management company about the renewal process and your interest in continuing your tenancy. They can provide specific information regarding lease renewal options and any factors influencing their decision.

In general, though, on-time payments, your rapport with the property manager and/or landlord, being a friendly neighbor, and maintaining the space are important in decision making:

>> On-time rent payments are critical to the maintenance and upkeep of the property. Landlords are aware of (and appreciate) tenants who make timely payments.

>> Treating the property manager (if applicable) and landlord with respect and being professional when contacting them about issues in your rental are very positive attributes that landlords pay attention to. (Chapter 10 has details on working well with a property manager.)

>> Tenants that get along peacefully with other tenants (if they live in an apartment building) and follow the lease's rules are ideal. Happy tenants make happy homes.

>> Keeping your space tidy and clean shows you care about the property and is a good sign of a healthy and happy tenant. (Flip to Chapter 10 for more info on the maintenance and repairs that tenants are typically responsible for.)

REMEMBER

Prioritizing a pleasant living experience and maintaining a responsible tenancy greatly contribute to your long-term leasing success.

Expecting a rent increase

Yes, you can expect rent increases in the rental market. Rent increases, though inconvenient, are related to the property's operation and maintenance:

>> **The rising cost of maintaining and operating the building or home:** Property taxes, utility expenses, insurance premiums, and the general cost of repairs and maintenance tend to increase over time. Landlords must cover these expenses to ensure that the property remains in good condition and provide tenants with a safe and comfortable living environment. As these costs rise annually, landlords often pass a portion of the burden onto tenants through rent increases.

>> **Inflation:** During periods of high inflation, the overall cost of goods and services rises faster. That includes materials and supplies necessary for property maintenance, repairs, and

renovations. To offset these increased costs and maintain the property's financial viability, landlords may increase rent.

>> **The rental market:** In areas with low inventory and high demand for rental properties, landlords may raise rents to keep up with the market average. This scenario is a reflection of supply and demand dynamics. Landlords want to ensure that their rental income aligns with market rates, especially in times of intense competition for available properties. By adjusting rents in line with the market rental rates, landlords can attract and retain tenants while ensuring their investment remains financially sustainable.

Rent increases should be within the legal limits set by local tenant laws and regulations. These laws vary by city and state and often outline the maximum allowable percentage for rent increases within a specific time frame. Knowing these regulations can help you understand your rights and responsibilities as a tenant.

REMEMBER

When you're faced with a rent increase, approach the situation proactively. Discuss it with your landlord to clearly understand the reasons behind the increase. Express any concerns or constraints and engage in open dialogue to explore possible alternatives or negotiate the terms. (See the following section for more about rent negotiation.) Ultimately, your rent increase may be unavoidable. By staying informed, proactive, and engaged in communication with your landlord, you can make informed decisions and make sure that the rent increase is fair and reasonable within the local rental market and your specific living situation.

Negotiating a better deal

TIP

Interested in negotiating a better rent amount before you renew your lease? Here are some suggestions to get started:

>> **Research the rental market in your area.** Conduct thorough research and understand the average rental rates for similar properties. This knowledge provides you with leverage and a solid foundation for negotiation.

>> **Highlight and showcase your strengths as a tenant.** If you have an excellent rental history, consistently pay rent on time, and maintain the property well, emphasize these qualities to your landlord. Demonstrating your reliability can strengthen your negotiation position.

>> **Determine your target price and set a realistic price based on your research and ability to pay your rent comfortably.** Figure out the maximum rent you're willing to pay and the ideal rent you want to achieve. These numbers help guide your negotiation strategy. Your landlord may have different numbers in mind, so be prepared to negotiate terms within your limits.

>> **Remember that rent isn't the only aspect you can negotiate.** Consider discussing lease terms such as the length of the lease, security deposit, included utilities, or any necessary repairs or upgrades. Being open to negotiating multiple rental agreement points can increase your chances of achieving a better deal overall.

>> **Offer incentives that may benefit the landlord to strengthen your position.** These items may include a longer lease term (as I discuss in the following section), prepaying a few months' rent in advance, or agreeing to take care of specific maintenance responsibilities like cleaning and sweeping a common area, taking out the trash, and taking care of some of the green space. These concessions demonstrate your commitment and make your offer more appealing.

WARNING

Timing is very, very important. Starting negotiations well before your lease renewal or when demand for rental properties is lower can provide more flexibility and room for negotiation. Waiting until the last minute may limit your options.

Make sure you approach communication and negotiations with a respectful and professional attitude. Explain your reasons for requesting a favorable rent and persuasively present your case. Keep the lines of communication open and listen to the landlord's perspective.

If you can't agree with your landlord, explore alternative options. That may involve searching for other rental properties that better fit your budget or considering a roommate (with landlord consent) to share the costs.

REMEMBER

Negotiation outcomes vary, and your success isn't guaranteed. However, by being well informed about rent prices; being prepared to negotiate; and maintaining a respectful, flexible, and proactive approach, you increase your chances of securing a better deal on your rent.

Signing a multiyear lease

In the wonderful world of rent negotiation (which I cover in the preceding section), some savvy tenants strategically request a multiyear lease of two to three years or more as part of their application process. By successfully negotiating the rent and locking in a desired affordable price, tenants can gain a victory that significantly impacts their financial well-being.

REMEMBER

You need to consider certain factors before signing on a multiyear lease agreement:

>> **Having strong savings is vital when committing to a multiyear lease.** Although this kind of lease offers the advantage of a locked-in, affordable price, unexpected circumstances can arise during the tenancy that may make that price suddenly less affordable. In the event of a job loss or unforeseen financial challenges, having substantial savings to draw from can help you navigate difficult situations without jeopardizing your ability to fulfill your lease obligations.

>> **Because a long-term lease extends over multiple years, you need to ensure that your source of income is secure.** This stability provides the reassurance that you'll be able to meet your financial obligations throughout the duration of the lease.

By demonstrating your stability, financial responsibility, and forward-thinking approach, you present yourself as an attractive tenant to landlords. This position increases your chances of successfully negotiating a multiyear lease.

WARNING

A multiyear lease is a commitment that you shouldn't take lightly. Carefully review the terms and conditions of the lease agreement and get clarification on any clauses related to rent increases, early termination, or potential penalties. Understanding the lease thoroughly lets you make an informed decision and ensures that you're comfortable with the long-term commitment.

You also need to maintain open lines of communication with your landlord throughout the tenancy. Discussing any changes in your circumstances or potential financial challenges as they arise can help foster a positive relationship and address any concerns.

In the following sections, I dig deeper into the advantages and disadvantages of signing a multiyear lease.

The pros

Signing a multiyear lease agreement offers multiple advantages for tenants:

>> **Provides stability and eliminates the uncertainty of annual lease renewals:** By committing to a longer lease term, you can engage in better long-term planning and enjoy the peace of mind that comes with having a fixed place to call home for an extended period. This feature is especially helpful for renters with long-term plans in the area, such as pursuing education, building a career, or starting a family. It eliminates the need to worry about frequent relocations, allowing them to establish roots in the community and enjoy a consistent living situation.

>> **May include a provision that locks in the rental rate:** This term protects tenants from potential rent increases in a volatile rental market, especially in areas with rising rental rates or high housing demand. By avoiding annual rent increases, you can better plan and allocate your budget, knowing your housing costs will remain steady.

>> **Reduces the hassle and costs associated with frequent moves:** You can avoid expenses related to hiring movers, changing utility services, and other relocation costs. Settling into a home and community fosters a sense of belonging and minimizes the disruption of frequent relocations.

>> **Fosters a stronger relationship with the landlord:** Both parties have the opportunity to develop understanding and trust, leading to improved communication, timely maintenance, and a more responsive landlord when issues arise.

The cons

WARNING

Signing a multiyear lease agreement can provide various benefits (as you find out in the preceding section), but you also need to consider the potential drawbacks:

>> **Lack of flexibility:** Negotiating a multiyear lease means committing to the rental property for a significant time. If

your circumstances change during that time, such as a job relocation or a need to adjust your living situation, breaking the lease without penalties or finding a replacement tenant can be challenging. This lack of flexibility can restrict your options in responding to life changes.

>> **Financial constraints:** The flip side of rent increase stability is that you must pay the agreed-upon rent for the entire duration. If your financial situation changes, such as a job loss or unexpected expenses, you may find renegotiating the terms or finding more affordable housing options difficult. This situation can lead to financial strain if you have trouble meeting the rent obligation.

Before you sign a multiyear lease, carefully evaluate your circumstances. Think about your income stream(s); will your income be secure for the duration of the lease term? Do you have savings in the event of a job loss or economic downturn?

>> **Change in the rental market:** Rental markets can be volatile, with fluctuations in demand and changing rental rates. By committing to a long-term lease, you may miss out on opportunities to take advantage of lower rental rates or find more desirable housing options during the lease term. Such a commitment can limit your ability to pivot to changing market conditions.

>> **Potential changes in landlord/ownership:** The owner of the property may sell it during the term of a multiyear lease. Every owner has a unique style of managing the building and working with the tenants, and these changes can impact your overall living experience. Closely consider how likely your rental is to change hands and how willing you are to be stuck with a new owner before committing to a long-term lease.

Moving On

Moving from your old place can be a mix of emotions and experiences. Cheers to moving on: It's a transition to a new chapter in your life and brings both excitement and nostalgia. Moving on signifies growth and the possibility of new experiences. In the following sections, I discuss your next steps to finish the transition from old to new.

Leaving on good terms

Leaving on good terms from your current rental is a positive approach that can help maintain a good relationship and favorable impression with your landlord or property manager. Former landlords can write favorable recommendations on your behalf and may even have other properties you may be interested in renting, so exiting on good terms is always a good thing.

REMEMBER

With the following tips, you can leave your current rental on a high note and maintain a positive relationship with your landlord or property management:

» **Carefully review your lease agreement to understand the terms and conditions regarding move-out procedures, notice periods, and any specific requirements or obligations.** Your lease agreement states how much advance notice you must give the landlord before you move out. Typically, this period is 30 to 60 days, but it may vary depending on local regulations or your lease terms. Providing ample notice shows respect for the landlord's time and allows them to plan for your departure.

» **Before moving out, thoroughly clean the rental to leave it in the best possible condition.** Clean all rooms, appliances, floors, and fixtures. Pay special attention to areas requiring extra cleaning, such as the kitchen and bathroom. Repair damages or minor issues you may have caused during your tenancy, such as nail holes or scuff marks on the walls. Returning the home in a clean, well-maintained state shows your responsibility as a tenant and helps ensure that you receive your full security deposit (as I explain in the following section).

» **Contact the landlord or property manager to ensure you've settled all outstanding balances for rent and additional fees and charges.** This way, you prevent any financial disputes. Keep records of payments and receipts as proof of payment.

» **Return all keys, access cards, or devices associated with the rental.** Make sure to get them back to the landlord or property management on time and per their instructions.

Getting back the money you're owed

Receiving your security deposit should be a smooth and easy process when you return your space in the same condition you rented it. Normal wear and tear is to be expected and shouldn't prevent you from receiving your full security deposit, but you do need to sweep the floors; clean the kitchen, bathroom(s), and walls; and make sure the appliances are functioning.

The following steps review how to receive your deposit back:

1. **Review your lease agreement and understand the terms and conditions for the deposit's return, including deadlines and requirements.**

2. **Document the rental unit's condition and take photos or videos of each room before moving out to capture any existing damages or issues.**

   This evidence is crucial in case of disputes.

3. **Contact the landlord and request a move-out inspection.**

   Be available for any inspections and final walk-through of the space.

4. **Complete your lease requirements such as cleaning and repairs.**

   Additionally, follow the lease agreement guidelines to ensure that you return the property in the same condition, accounting for normal wear and tear.

5. **Provide proper move-out notice as stated in your lease agreement to avoid penalties or deductions from your deposit.**

6. **Request in writing that your landlord or property management company return your security deposit.**

   Clearly state the expected refund amount and provide a mailing address.

7. **Follow up if you don't receive a response within a reasonable time frame.**

   Send a polite reminder through written correspondence, such as email or certified mail.

8. **Understand local laws regarding deposit return.**

   Reach out to your real estate agent to get clarity on security deposit laws and regulations, including specific timelines for returns or requirements for itemized deductions.

9. **Speak with a real estate attorney if your attempts to recover the deposit are unsuccessful.**

   Also consider consulting with a local tenant rights organization to understand your rights and to take further action.

REMEMBER

Be sure to keep copies of all correspondence, receipts, and documentation related to the security deposit. Following these steps, staying organized, and maintaining open communication can improve your chances of successfully recovering your security deposit.

Knowing what happens when you break your lease early

WARNING

Your lease is a legally binding document, and breaking it has serious consequences. You may be required to pay a penalty or early termination fee. This fee can vary, but it's usually a certain number of months' rent or a fixed amount (it's stated in your lease agreement). Additionally, you may still be liable for paying rent until the landlord finds a new tenant to move in.

Breaking a lease also may result in the loss of your security deposit. Landlords often use the security deposit to cover unpaid rent, damages, or expenses incurred during this process. Be prepared to forfeit all or a portion of it if the landlord can't find a suitable tenant in a timely manner.

A broken lease can impact your rental history and make securing future rentals challenging (because landlords sometimes share this information with other landlords). Landlords may view a broken lease as a sign of potential financial risk.

In some cases, landlords may even pursue legal action to recover any financial losses incurred because you broke the lease early. This situation can result in additional expenses, such as legal fees, if a judgment is made against you.

REMEMBER

The consequences of breaking a lease early can vary depending on the state and city you live in, the terms of your lease agreement, and the cooperation of your landlord. Some landlords are flexible and understanding, and some aren't. I highly recommend that you review your lease agreement and communicate with your landlord as soon as possible if you're considering breaking your lease. Discussing your situation and potential solutions with the landlord can help lessen the financial impact and find a resolution that works for both parties.

4

Enjoying Life in Your Own Place

Chapter **12**

Following the Rules and Staying Safe

Your safety and the safety of any other occupants in your rental home are paramount. In this chapter I discuss the importance of following your rental's rules and regulations — and what happens when you don't. I also provide some pointers on staying safe.

Knowing That Rental Rules Aren't Meant to Be Broken

Despite the common saying, your rental's rules are there for a reason — especially those that involve people's well-being and safety.

Many rentals have shared areas like parking spaces, lobbies, hallways, and elevators. House rules help regulate the use of these shared spaces, ensuring that they remain clean, well maintained, and accessible for every tenant. These guidelines can include regulations on locking doors, being mindful of visitors, or reporting suspicious activities.

Obeying house rules promotes fairness and consideration among residents, helps create a secure living environment, and protects the well-being of the residents.

REMEMBER

For the record, I'm using the term *house rules* to refer to the guidelines of any type of rental property — house, apartment, condo, and so on.

House rules also outline responsibilities for property maintenance and cleanliness, including trash disposal, noise levels, and guarding against activities that can damage the property (see Chapter 10 for more about repairs and maintenance). By following these rules, residents contribute to the upkeep and life span of the building.

REMEMBER

A rental's house rules often align with local and state laws and municipal building codes. They ensure that the property complies with legal requirements and safety standards. Following these rules protects the residents and the management from legal issues and liabilities.

In the following sections, I describe a few common rules for rental spaces and explain what happens when you don't follow the regulations.

TIP

Request a copy of the house rules from the landlord or property manager so that you always have them handy.

Looking at typical rental guidelines

The primary purpose of common rental rules is to ensure that all tenants can have a peaceful living space and enjoy clean, well-maintained common areas. These rules often cover issues like parking, visitor policies, and the proper use of common areas to ensure everyone can access and enjoy the building's facilities equally. They also frequently regulate noise levels within units as well as terms for subletting.

The following sections address typical rental rules and the consequences for violating them.

TIP

Rental rules may also address pet policies, specifying rules for pet ownership, leash requirements, and cleaning up after pets. Flip to Chapter 9 for more about living with a pet in your rental.

Parking in acceptable places

Parking rules specify designated parking areas, whether assigned spaces or entire parking lots. Adhering to these parking rules helps prevent congestion, allows efficient traffic flow, and ensures that parking spaces are fairly distributed among residents.

Park only in authorized areas and avoid blocking access points, fire lanes, or emergency exits. Additionally, make sure any guests or visitors follow permit regulations if applicable to prevent unauthorized vehicles from occupying resident spaces.

By respecting these rules and parking in designated areas, residents contribute to a well-organized parking system, reduce conflicts among neighbors, and enhance the overall living experience for all residents.

Parking in spaces or areas not designated for parking can result in a tow or fine.

Using common spaces

Common spaces are for the enjoyment of all residents. Avoid engaging in activities that may disturb or inconvenience other residents. Be mindful of noise levels, especially during quiet hours, to ensure a peaceful living space for everyone.

Being considerate, respectful, and tidy in your rental's common areas goes a long way toward creating a peaceful and harmonious community.

Avoid taking over any common area for extended periods. Consider other residents' needs and preferences, such as sharing seating areas and exercise equipment.

As you're using and moving about the common spaces, pay close attention to any posted rules or signs for using common areas, such as restrictions on hours, specific activities, and guest policies.

If you see any maintenance issues or damage in the common areas, report them to the property manager or the landlord. Help maintain the cleanliness and condition of the shared spaces by throwing away trash and using facilities with care.

Tossing your unit's trash and recycling

Properly disposing of trash and recycling from your rental is vital for maintaining cleanliness, caring for the environment, and promoting sustainability. Follow any instructions provided by your building management regarding trash and recycling procedures.

Make sure to stay informed about any changes in recycling guidelines or trash policies. Be aware of any special recycling events or initiatives in your area and follow any instructions your building management provides regarding trash and recycling procedures. Check your local recycling authority's website for detailed information.

WARNING

Some lease agreements and *riders* (which state any additional terms not in the lease) specify fines and penalties for not disposing of trash and recycling properly. I cover leases and riders in more detail in Chapter 6.

TIP

If your landlord or property manager doesn't specify trash or recycling disposal guidelines, I recommend this easy process:

1. **Install two trash bins lined with plastic bags in your rental — a black bag for trash and a clear bag for recycling.**

    Label each container to avoid confusion.

2. **Separate recyclable items such as paper, plastic, glass, and metal from your trash.**

    Before placing items in the recycling bin, rinse containers, remove lids, and flatten cardboard boxes to save space.

    Properly clean and empty any food waste from items before disposing of them in the trash.

3. **Securely tie the bags to prevent spills and odors when emptying your bins.**

4. **Place the full bags in designated bins or chute areas per your rental's rules.**

    Avoid overloading the containers to prevent overflowing and pests.

Hosting visitors

Hosting visitors is a great way to socialize and create lasting memories, as long as you do it responsibly and respectfully.

TIP

Here are some tips on how to have fun with hosting and do it with care:

» **Inform your neighbors beforehand about your plans to have guests over, especially if you anticipate a larger gathering.** Doing so shows you're considerate and allows neighbors to plan accordingly.

» **Review the rental's rules and regulations regarding guests.** Some apartments have specific guidelines on the number of guests permitted, the quiet hours, and common area usage. Make sure you're following the rules pertaining to gatherings.

» **Be aware of noise levels, especially during any designated quiet hours.** Keep the volume of music, conversations, and other activities low to avoid disturbing your neighbors.

Head to the later section "Keeping down the noise" for more on sound considerations.

» **If your building has limited parking spaces, encourage visitors to carpool or take public transportation or a rideshare to the gathering.**

» **Discuss with your guests the building's rules and expectations.** Your guests are just as responsible for using designated smoking areas, respecting common areas, keeping noise down, and following parking regulations as you are.

Letting them know about house rules ahead of time helps them understand and follow them.

By making sure that your guests follow house rules, you create an enjoyable experience for everyone involved. Your neighbors will appreciate it, and you maintain a peaceful and tranquil environment. I consider this a win–win!

Subletting your rental

Subletting your rental occurs when you turn around and rent the residence you've rented to someone else. It's a viable option if you need to move out temporarily but want to retain the lease.

Although subletting is risky and requires prior approval from your landlord, doing it correctly can provide you with a temporary resident to cover your rent.

WARNING

When you sublet your rental, you remain liable for the rent.

Carefully review your lease agreement (see Chapter 6) to understand whether it allows subletting. Some leases include language that prohibits subletting or have specific requirements and procedures to follow. You need to follow the guidelines outlined in your lease.

Generally speaking, though, here's how the subletting process works:

1. **Contact your landlord or property management company to seek their permission for subletting.**

   Getting written consent from the landlord or manager before proceeding is crucial.

2. **After you have the decision maker's permission in writing, contact your rental agent to begin marketing the space.**

   You must confirm with the agent that you've received permission to sublet the apartment.

REMEMBER

Your agent then advertises your place for sublet through various platforms such as online listing websites, social media, and digital ads. The ad should provide precise details about the length of the sublease, rent amount, any furnished or unfurnished options, and any specific requirements or restrictions such the smoking policy and any pet restrictions.

If you don't hire an agent to help you with this process, you can advertise your place on different platforms yourself.

TIP

The agent gathers the required documentation, such as the proposed subtenant's background information, credit rating, proof of income, verified assets, and references. They carefully screen potential candidates on your behalf to make sure you get to select a reliable and responsible one.

3. After you've found a suitable subtenant, submit their documentation to the landlord for review and approval.

4. After your candidate is approved, have your agent draft a sublease agreement.

This document should outline the sublease terms, including the duration, rent amount, responsibilities, and specific rules or conditions. I recommend that your agent use a standardized sublease agreement template and rider to ensure that all necessary provisions are included.

You can read more about leases and riders in Chapter 6.

TIP

If you're subletting without the help of an agent, you can check out this site for help: https://eforms.com/rental/.

REMEMBER

Request a security deposit from the subtenant, equivalent to one month's rent, to protect against any damages or unpaid rent. Follow the legal guidelines in your area regarding the handling and return of security deposits. A helpful website is www.rocketlawyer.com/real-estate/landlords/property-management/legal-guide/security-deposit-laws-by-state.

5. Before the subtenant moves in, conduct a thorough walkthrough of the apartment together.

Note the unit's condition and document, photograph, and take videos of any existing damages or issues.

Create an inventory list of any furnishings or appliances in the sublease agreement.

6. Constantly communicate with your landlord and the subtenant during the sublease period.

Ensure that the subtenant makes rent payments promptly and that the property manager quickly reports and addresses any maintenance or repairs.

Create a reminder for the end date of the sublease and make necessary arrangements for your move-in when the sublease period is over. Communicate with your subtenant well in advance to ensure a smooth transition and make arrangements for key returns and any necessary cleaning or repairs.

REMEMBER

Subletting can be risky. However, you can mitigate the risk by following the rules, getting your landlord's approval, and hiring a qualified rental agent to find a suitable renter. Good luck!

Keeping down the noise

Every resident has a fundamental right to peaceful enjoyment in their space. That means they're entitled to use and enjoy their rental property without interference from the landlord or other tenants. This prerogative includes the right to privacy, freedom from unreasonable disturbances, and the ability to reside on the premises peacefully.

TIP

Maintaining a reasonable noise level is crucial when living with other residents. Consistent loud noises are what residents complain about the most. Noise issues can cause friction among residents and an uncomfortable living experience. What's reasonable? A good noise level is speaking in a conversational tone or playing music at a level that doesn't travel from your space into a common hall or neighboring home.

Other noise-level offenders include loud parties, construction or repairs that cause excessive noise, or any other activities that interfere with the peaceful enjoyment of the rental. If nuisances occur, tenants can report them to the landlord or the property manager.

WARNING

If you consistently violate another tenant's right to quiet and peaceful living, they may have legal recourse. This avenue may involve filing a complaint with the landlord, seeking mediation or arbitration, or even taking legal action to enforce their rights.

If you suspect the noise level in your apartment may be an issue, reach out to your neighbors to inquire about it. Make them aware that you're considerate about the noise level and that they should reach out to you if it's too loud at any time.

TIP

Here are a few tips to ensure you're doing all you can to keep the noise level down in your rental:

>> **Find out about the designated quiet hours.** These hours are usually during the evening and nighttime when residents are more likely to rest or sleep.

During these hours, avoid activities that create excessive noise, such as playing loud music, moving furniture, or using loud appliances like blenders, vacuum cleaners, or washing machines.

>> **Proactively consider your neighbors' needs for a quiet living environment.** Inform them if you plan to host a gathering or have a situation that may cause temporary noise.

Showing consideration and addressing concerns can help create a friendly and understanding relationship.

>> **When watching TV, listening to music, or playing instruments, use headphones or invest in soundproofing materials.** These items can help muffle the noise and prevent it from spreading to neighbors.

>> **In apartments, use a rug or carpet in the living room and bedrooms if you have wood floors.** Floor coverings can help absorb sound and reduce the impact of footsteps or other noise caused by walking or moving furniture.

REMEMBER

Being aware of the impact of your activities and showing consideration for your neighbors can help create a peaceful and harmonious living environment in your apartment. Good communication and mutual respect are vital to maintaining positive relationships with your neighbors and ensuring a quiet atmosphere for everyone.

Facing the consequences when you break a rule

The consequences for breaking the rental rules your landlord sets can vary depending on the violation and the terms in your lease agreement or the building's regulations.

If you break a rule for the first time, your landlord or property manager may issue a written warning. This communication serves as a notice of the violation and a reminder to follow the rules. It states the rule you've broken and may provide information on possible consequences if the behavior continues.

You may also receive a fine or penalty depending on the severity of the rule violation.

Some violations may result in losing privileges to specific amenities or common areas. For example, if you consistently violate noise rules, you may be prohibited from using spaces like the gym or shared outdoor areas. This punishment is intended to encourage compliance with the building rules.

If your behavior severely or consistently disrupts the quiet enjoyment of other residents, causes damage to the property, or violates the terms of your lease, your landlord may choose to terminate your tenancy and evict you. They may even pursue legal action if the violations persist despite warnings and fines.

WARNING

You don't want your landlord to have to resort to legal action. It's costly and time consuming, and it can end up on your credit report as a landlord-tenant dispute, making renting another place difficult.

REMEMBER

Take steps to resolve any building violations before it reaches the lawsuit stage. If you're facing the results of a rule violation, communicate with your landlord or property manager, take responsibility for your actions, and work toward resolving the issues.

Staying Safe When Living in Close Quarters with Others

Be alert to your surroundings and prioritize the safety and well-being of yourself and others when living in a shared rented space. The following sections provide some important guidelines.

Being prepared for fires and other emergencies

Fire and emergency preparedness probably immediately come to mind when you consider safety in your home. Whether you live in a large apartment complex, a single-family rental home, or a small apartment building, understanding how to decrease the chances of experiencing a significant emergency and knowing what to do if one presents itself are essential to living safely.

REMEMBER

Memorize your property's fire safety procedures, including the location of fire exits, fire extinguishers, and smoke detectors. Knowing where emergency exits are located and understanding your building's plan of action in a major fire can be the difference between evacuating unscathed and being trapped in a burning building. If a fire occurs, don't take the elevators; proceed to the nearest staircase.

Don't do things like the following that jeopardize your and other residents' fire safety and well-being:

>> Forgetting to turn off the stove or oven

>> Burning candles in an unoccupied apartment

>> Leaving running space heaters unattended

>> Failing to report faulty electrical wiring

>> Letting the batteries in your smoke detector(s) die

>> Creating fire hazards, such as storing shoe or coat racks in common hallways or anywhere that blocks your walkway

TIP

Create a checklist of things to turn off and check before leaving the rental. Attach the list to your refrigerator or place it in another prominent location that will remind you to do a safety check on these items.

Speak with your property manager or landlord about emergency procedures during a fire, natural disaster, medical emergency, or power outage. Keep emergency contact numbers, including building management and maintenance staff, ready and in an easy-to-find place.

TIP

Consider creating an emergency kit with essential supplies like first aid items, flashlights, bottles of water, and nonperishable food.

Making sure to lock doors and windows

You can never be too careful regarding security in your home. Locking your doors and windows is one of the most effective ways to keep yourself and other tenants safe, prevent theft, and keep unwanted strangers from entering the property. Securing your apartment is a deterrent to potential intruders.

TIP

Develop a habit of locking doors and windows whenever you leave your place, even for just a short period. By doing so, you contribute to the overall safety and security of yourself and your rental. In fact, you may want to lock all entry points even when you're *inside.*

Here are a few guidelines to remember when entering and leaving your home:

>> Be cautious when allowing visitors into the building.

>> Don't prop open doors or allow strangers to enter without ID or authorization.

>> Contact the landlord or property manager to report suspicious activity (as I explain later in this chapter).

>> Check all the doors and windows to make sure they have sturdy locks. If they don't, contact your landlord, property manager, or maintenance department for help.

Becoming familiar with your neighbors

Getting to know your neighbors, at least by sight, helps promote community in an apartment building by fostering better relationships, increased trust, and a willingness to look out for one another's safety. Knowing the people around you also contributes to a safer living environment.

When you become familiar with your neighbors and their routines, you can more easily recognize suspicious activity. If you notice someone out of the ordinary, you can quickly notify the property manager or the police, which can help prevent potential crimes or damage to the property.

Knowing your neighbors can also provide strong communication during emergencies. In situations like fire alarms, building maintenance issues, or community updates, you can relay information quickly to ensure everyone's safety and well-being.

Reporting something suspicious

If you notice something unusual or suspicious anywhere near your rental home, take a moment to assess the situation. Pay attention to details such as the description of individuals involved, their behavior, and any relevant information that can help authorities or building management.

If you believe a situation is an immediate threat to you, another resident, or the property, contact 911 immediately. Then reach out to your landlord or property manager to alert them of the situation.

REMEMBER

Per the Department of Homeland Security, if you see something suspicious, you should always call local law enforcement and do the following:

» If it's a life-threatening emergency, call 911.

» When reporting suspicious activity, give the most accurate description possible, including as much of the following info as you can:

- Brief description of the activity
- Date, time, and location of the activity
- Physical identifiers of anyone you observed
- Descriptions of vehicles
- Information about where people involved in suspicious activities may have gone
- Your name and contact information (optional)

Visit www.dhs.gov/see-something-say-something/how-to-report-suspicious-activity for more information.

REMEMBER

Reporting something suspicious is a responsible action that can help prevent potential threats or crimes. If you see something, say something. It keeps not only you but also your community safe.

Chapter **13**

Decorating Do's and Don'ts

You have the power to turn your rental into a genuinely impressive and inviting living space with furniture and decor. With a dash of creativity and a sprinkle of planning, you can elevate the comfort and style of your humble abode.

So let your imagination run wild, explore new possibilities, and embark on this exciting journey of transforming your rental into a place you'll love to call home.

With the help of this chapter, get ready to create a space that reflects your personality and brings a smile every time you walk through the door.

Making Cosmetic Changes to Your Place (If You're Allowed)

Making cosmetic changes to your apartment or rental house can be fun and rewarding. It allows you to personalize your living space and create an environment that reflects your style and radiates positive energy.

Cosmetic changes include things like painting, changing fixtures (including lighting), adding trim and moldings, adding a tile backsplash, hanging shelves, and replacing the bathroom vanity.

Your lease (see Chapter 6) likely has language that prohibits any upgrades without prior notice, so you should always seek permission from your landlord or property manager before making cosmetic changes. Make sure that you get the approval in writing.

Your landlord will require you to use someone licensed and insured to perform the work. In fact, they may insist you use their preferred licensed contractor, electrician, plumber, and/or carpenter for any approved modifications and upgrades.

Be prepared to have the work done during the hours the landlord or property manager sets out so that it doesn't inconvenience other residents.

In most cases, you, not the landlord, cover labor and material costs related to these upgrades or changes. However, you and the landlord must determine what happens to the upgrades when you leave the rental. Do you have to paint the walls back to their original color? Do the new fixtures stay, or do you take them with you?

If the enhancements add value to the unit, the landlord will most likely approve the changes and request that they stay with the unit. Or you may suggest upfront that your improvements remain with the unit, thus increasing the odds of the work being approved.

Whatever the decision, what happens at the end of your lease must be agreed to in writing and included in an addition in your lease agreement.

I recommend that you wait at least six months after moving into your space to request cosmetic upgrades; you may even consider waiting until after you renew your lease.

Before taking on any cosmetic changes, make sure you can cover any related cost of returning the space to its original state if that's what the landlord wants. Be sure to store away any original fixtures or items you replace to ensure that you can restore the space to its original condition when needed.

Styling Your Rental, or at Least Making Sure Everything Fits

Decorating and furnishing your rental home can be a gratifying and exciting process. One of the joys of renting a space is the opportunity to define your home in your vision and aesthetic.

The following sections walk you through the process.

Deciding on a look upfront

If you're keen on interior design, start by deciding your style or theme for the space. Research various styles, such as modern, minimalist, traditional, eclectic, and contemporary, online and see what appeals to you. This information can guide you when you're choosing furniture, colors, patterns, and accessories.

TIP

I recommend the following resources as you decide on a style for your rental:

>> Magazines such as *Elle Décor* (www.elledecor.com) and *House Beautiful* (www.housebeautiful.com) can be sources of inspiration.

>> I also like Apartment Therapy (www.apartmenttherapy. com/), Style by Emily Henderson (https://stylebyemily henderson.com/), and MyDomaine (www.mydomaine.com/).

>> Pinterest (www.pinterest.com) is also a great source of ideas.

Measuring to make sure everything fits

Imagine a world where your furniture fits perfectly in your home, creating a cozy space you absolutely love. Well, guess what? You can make that dream a reality by following a few simple steps!

Whether you're arranging furniture you already own or furnishing your place from scratch, taking precise measurements is essential for ensuring that your pieces fit seamlessly within your home.

Here I walk you through the step-by-step process of measuring a room and furniture to help you make informed decisions:

1. **Use your tape measure and measure the length and width of the room — in feet and inches — you're working in.**

   Write these figures down or put them in the notes app on your phone.

TIP

2. **Pay attention to any architectural features that may impact or disrupt furniture placement, such as windows, doors, and alcoves.**

   These details help you start to visualize how different pieces fit into the room. Measure the dimensions of these features and note them, too.

3. **Measure clearances for doorways, hallways, and other high-traffic areas.**

   Take into account the flow of traffic within the room and allow enough space for easy movement. Doing so ensures that you can easily maneuver furniture without limiting mobility or creating cramped rooms or areas.

4. **If you have existing furniture you plan to use in the room, measure each piece's dimensions.**

   This step is vital to determine whether your current furniture fits. Knowing the measurements of your existing pieces helps you figure out how they'll interact with any new additions and gauge the space for additional items.

5. **Measure the width and height of building doorways, stairwells, elevators, and any other entry points the furniture needs to pass.**

   This critical step helps you avoid the frustration of struggling to fit oversized furniture through narrow passages or, worse, not being able to get the pieces in the door at all.

6. **Create a floor plan to visualize the furniture placement and the space flow.**

   You can use an app or a pen and paper for this step. Arrange the furniture to maximize functionality and allow for comfortable movement.

Picking useful pieces

Start with choosing essential furniture pieces based on your needs, your budget, and the size of the rooms. (Check out the following section for tips on finding pieces for cheap.)

These items may include a sofa or sectional, coffee table, dining table, chairs, beds, and storage units. Choose pieces that fit your priorities, whether that's style, practicality, comfort, functionality, or whatever.

TIP

When selecting new furniture for a room in your rental, you may want to consider the scale and proportion of the pieces to the room size. Oversized furniture in a small room can make the space feel cramped, while small furniture in a large room may appear disproportionate. I cover the ins and outs of room and furniture measurement in the preceding section.

Making your space more stylish

Examine the space's size and natural lighting as well as your personal preferences. Choose colors that complement each other and create an inviting atmosphere while sticking to your preferred style (see the earlier section "Deciding on a look upfront"). You can add pops of color through accessories and accent pieces.

TIP

Pay close attention to the lighting. Lighting is vital in every room and significantly impacts the room's ambiance. Consider using ceiling lights, floor lamps, table lamps, and wall sconces strategically to create a bright, cheerful, and inviting space.

You can be bold and creative by adding attractive decorative accessories. Consider pillows, rugs, curtains, artwork, mirrors, plants, and other pieces you like. Strategic choices with these pieces bring character and texture to the room. (Get the scoop on hanging artwork and other wall decor later in this chapter.)

WARNING

Don't clutter the space by adding too many items, though. Maintain the area's balance and ensure that each addition complements the room's overall look to create a pleasant and harmonious environment.

Have fun and be adventurous when mixing furniture styles and materials in your living space. Don't be afraid to experiment and create a unique and eclectic look. By combining different textures, patterns, and finishes, you can add visual excitement to the room. Just make sure the different elements work together cohesively, creating a pleasing overall composition. I encourage you to unleash your creativity and let your living space reflect your style!

For the finishing touches, include storage bins to keep your living space organized and clutter-free. Choose furniture with built-in storage compartments, invest in stylish storage baskets or containers, and use vertical space with shelves or wall-mounted organizers.

Then blend your personality into the room by displaying meaningful items, paintings, and pictures that evoke positive emotions. Incorporate personal items that express your interests, hobbies, and travels. This personalization adds character and makes the space feel uniquely yours.

Take your time, trust your instincts, and create a space that makes you feel comfortable, happy, and proud. Welcome home!

Finding inexpensive furniture and decor

You have plenty of options for finding inexpensive furniture and decor for your home if you're willing to exercise patience and resourcefulness. Check out the following tips:

>> One great place to start is thrift stores and consignment shops, where you can discover secondhand furniture at affordable prices. These stores often boast unique and vintage pieces that may perfectly align with your style and budget.

>> Another category worth exploring is online marketplaces such as Craigslist, Facebook Marketplace, and OfferUp. These platforms allow people to sell their used furniture at lower prices. By searching local listings and engaging in negotiations, you can secure a fantastic deal that meets your requirements.

>> If you enjoy the thrill of hunting for hidden treasures, don't overlook garage sales and estate sales. These events can offer many discounted furniture items waiting to be discovered.

Keep your eyes open for signs posted in your neighborhood, or search the web for upcoming sales in your area.

>> Don't forget big-box stores like IKEA, Big Lots, Target, and Walmart. These places offer budget-conscious furniture options that cater to a wide range of styles and designs. With their variety of selections, you're sure to find affordable pieces that align with your taste and vision for your home.

>> If you prefer online shopping to crowded stores and waiting in lines, companies like Wayfair, Overstock, and Amazon offer large collections of lower-priced furniture. These online platforms consistently provide discounts and deals, making finding inexpensive pieces that perfectly suit your aesthetic preferences easy.

Before making an online purchase, make sure you read online reviews of your top choice. Be sure that past customer experiences from start to finish are satisfactory.

>> If you're looking for short-term furnishing solutions or experimenting with different styles, furniture rental companies like Feather (if you live in New York City, Los Angeles, or San Francisco; https://livefeather.com) or CORT Furniture Rental (www.cort.com) offer cost-friendly options.

I've used both companies and found their processes seamless and affordable, allowing for stress-free temporary furniture arrangements.

>> Explore local buy/sell/trade groups on social media platforms or community forums. These groups often serve as hubs for individuals selling gently used furniture at lower prices. You never know what hidden gems you may find within these online communities.

>> Keep an eye on clearance sections and sales at furniture stores. Seasonal sales and dedicated clearance sections can offer discounted furniture pieces that fit your budget.

As always, before making any purchase, inspect the condition of the furniture, carefully measure your space accurately (as I explain earlier in this chapter), and consider your style and needs.

Arranging Wall Decor

Hanging artwork and other wall decor requires precision and skill. When I need assistance and guidance with hanging major pieces, I often hire professionals through platforms like TaskRabbit (www. taskrabbit.com) and Thumbtack (www.thumbtack.com). However, hanging a collection of art or a single statement piece all by yourself can be easier than you think.

First things first: Where do you want your piece to go? Here are some options:

>> **At eye level:** Typically, a person's line of sight is 60 inches above the ground. You want the center of your piece to sit here, as shown in Figure 13-1. However, you can adjust this measurement according to your own height or personal preferences.

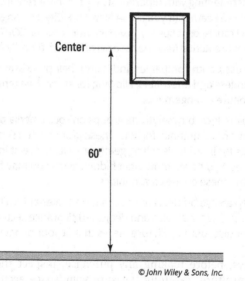

© John Wiley & Sons, Inc.

FIGURE 13-1: Hanging a piece at eye level.

>> **Above a sofa:** Make sure to have six to eight inches of space between the top of the sofa and the bottom of the piece. The width of the piece should be no more than two-thirds of the sofa's total length. See Figure 13-2.

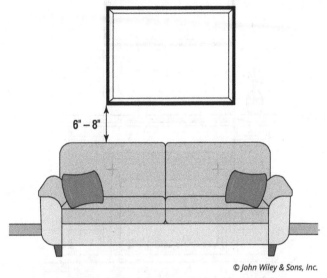

The width of the piece should be no more than two-thirds of the sofa's total length.

6" – 8"

© John Wiley & Sons, Inc.

FIGURE 13-2: Hanging a piece above a sofa.

>> **Above a fireplace:** Do you have a fireplace in your rental home? You're lucky! It's a natural place to hang decor. A piece looks best when it's wider than the fireplace's opening but no wider than the mantel, as Figure 13-3 illustrates.

A popular option for hanging multiple pieces is a gallery wall, whether that's pieces that are all the same size or pieces of different sizes. Check out Figure 13-4 for each of these options.

TIP

For the latter option, think of all the smaller items as one large picture. Start with the largest piece and arrange the smaller pieces around it.

In any type of gallery display, leave at least two inches of space between each piece and put your gallery's center at eye level.

Depending on the type of surface you're hanging a piece on, you may need tools beyond a hammer and nail:

>> On drywall, use drywall anchors and a drill.

>> On plaster, use nails with a drill.

>> On brick, use either brick clips or hard wall hangers.

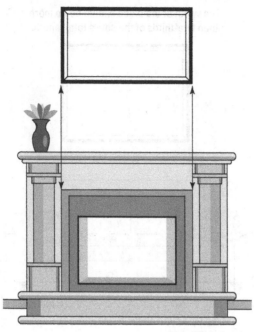

© John Wiley & Sons, Inc.

FIGURE 13-3: Hanging a piece above a fireplace.

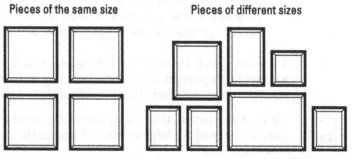

Pieces of the same size   Pieces of different sizes

© John Wiley & Sons, Inc.

FIGURE 13-4: Putting together a gallery.

But no matter what, don't forget to use a level! This tool is great for making sure your pieces are hung evenly, not crookedly.

Keep in mind that you may not be able to put any holes in your walls, depending on whether your landlord allows cosmetic changes, as I explain in the earlier section "Making Cosmetic Changes to Your Place (If You're Allowed)." If that's the case, consider using adhesive strips or hook and eye strips that you can easily remove at the end of your lease. These options are also good for hanging canvas pieces.

Adding Easy Upgrades to Your Rental

When upgrading your apartment, start by obtaining written approval from your landlord or property manager; for details, head to the earlier section "Making Cosmetic Changes to Your Place (If You're Allowed)." When you're ready to move out, be ready to change everything back to the way it was unless the landlord or property manager approved your upgrades as permanent.

With that important step taken care of, you can focus on the fun and exciting part of the process. Here are several ideas to consider toward upgrading your apartment:

>> **Paint:** Painting can work wonders in turning a dull, uninspiring room into a vibrant, inviting space that radiates light and openness.

Choose colors that complement your furniture and reflect your excellent style. Go for neutral tones to create a timeless and inspiring backdrop, or go bold with accent walls to add a pop of color. Be creative and have fun with it.

>> **Knobs and handles:** Say goodbye to boring handles and knobs and hello to a fresh look. By swapping these items out with options that match your style, you can easily upgrade the appearance of your kitchen and bathroom cabinets. This simple change adds a personalized touch to your space, giving even older cabinets a transformation.

Be sure to keep the original knobs handy so you can easily swap them back in if necessary when you move out.

>> **Lighting:** The lighting fixtures can add style and ambiance to any home. You can swap out an existing fixture for a pendant light, floor lamp, or task lighting to effectively illuminate specific areas, providing form, function, and aesthetic appeal.

Then choose energy-efficient LED bulbs to optimize energy use and reduce electricity costs. They offer long-lasting performance and contribute to a more sustainable and environmentally friendly lifestyle.

>> **Faucets:** Swap out an outdated bathroom or kitchen faucet with a water-efficient model that enhances functionality and adds a touch of your style. With this small change, you can give your bathroom or kitchen a fresh and updated look.

Search for fixtures that complement the room's aesthetic.

>> **Shower head:** Look for options that provide a refreshing and invigorating water flow. Choose water-saving features that help you conserve water without sacrificing the comfort and enjoyment of your showers.

For a spa-like feeling every time you step into the shower, consider a high-pressure or rain shower head. Pure bliss!

>> **Bathroom sink:** Another upgrade to consider is replacing the bathroom sink, although many landlords may not let you go that far.

A more stylish and functional sink can enhance your bathroom's visual appeal and functionality. My favorites are styles that prioritize storage space, providing adequate room to store toiletries and other bathroom items.

Ensure that the sink you choose matches your bathroom's style, creating a cohesive flow. This simple upgrade can make a huge difference in the look and usability of your bathroom space.

>> **Floors:** One of my personal favorite ways to add flavor to your tile is peel-and-stick flooring, available at most home improvement stores and online. Peel-and-stick tiles are generally affordable, especially for a smaller area like a bathroom or a small kitchen.

In most cases, you need at least two boxes of tiles to complete the project. The best part is that you may be able to accomplish this affordable upgrade in just one afternoon.

On the other hand, if you prefer to leave it to the pros, you can always rely on skilled installers for a polished finish.

TIP

Note that peel-and-stick flooring is reversible, although you may need to use a product like Goo Gone to remove any residual adhesive before moving out. If you execute the installation exceptionally well, however, your landlord may consider keeping the tiles in place when you leave.

If your landlord has approved this upgrade on the condition that you'll return it to the original tile and then you can't clear the peel-and-stick, you may be liable for damages and monies deducted from your security deposit.

>> **Smart devices:** You can enjoy convenience and efficiency benefits by incorporating smart home devices such as a programmable thermostat, intelligent lighting, or a voice-controlled virtual assistant.

Imagine controlling your home's temperature directly from your smartphone or effortlessly turning your lights on and off with a simple tap on your phone screen or speaking your command into your phone. These incredible advancements of technology make your daily life easier and add a touch of modernity, sophistication, and more connected living to your place.

As I note earlier in the chapter, you may well be footing the bill for upgrades that you can't take with you when you move out. Keep that in mind as you decide whether/what upgrades to splash out for.

5

The Part of Tens

Discover ten important facts to know when your apartment building is being sold.

Find out nearly ten crucial pieces of information about government subsidies and your rent.

Understand almost ten tasks your agent performs during your rental search.

Chapter **14**

Ten Things That Occur When Your Rental Is Sold

Suppose you're living happily in your rental home, and then all of a sudden, the unthinkable occurs: The landlord puts it on the market. What do you do now?

In this chapter you find out what happens when the rental you live in is being sold.

REMEMBER

To ensure that you understand your rights, I encourage you to carefully review your lease agreement, including critical information such as lease duration, rent terms, and any clauses related to property sales. Being crystal clear about the details of your lease agreement is pivotal in protecting your rights and responsibilities as a tenant throughout a property sale and empowers you to confidently navigate the situation and make informed decisions that serve your best interests.

Your Current Lease Remains Valid No Matter What

Just when you thought everything was settled after signing the lease for your dream rental, you get an email from the owner or property manager announcing that the rental property you live in is now for sale. You still have ten months left on your current lease; you've already invested in furniture and gotten to know the neighborhood. Now what?

REMEMBER

Your lease terms remain valid and your rent stays unchanged. The current owner is obligated to honor the terms and conditions of your lease for the duration you originally signed.

Your Rent May Go Up If You Renew Your Lease

Before your lease term concludes, the outgoing landlord may offer a lease renewal, which may involve a rent increase. Why? The person buying the building may want that unit occupied and may want the outgoing landlord to offer a renewal to the tenant at a higher rent or at the current market rate.

REMEMBER

One crucial aspect of an investment property is the monthly rent it generates. If your rent is lower than the current market rate, expiring leases can be valuable. New owners often seek market-rate rents from reliable tenants, so be prepared for your rent to go up under new ownership in this scenario.

Consider asking questions about the current owner's intentions regarding a potential sale before you sign the lease. Review the lease terms to understand how a sale affects your tenancy.

You Can Request Written Documentation About Your Lease

If you ever feel uncomfortable about the terms of your lease when the property is up for sale, don't hesitate to contact the owner or property manager. You can request assurance in writing that the remainder of your lease will continue until it naturally expires or a renewal is offered. (*Note:* Depending on your lease and city and state, your renewal rights vary upon the lease's expiration.) I've had many situations where tenants have come to me to discuss their rights and their lease while the buildings they live in are for sale.

The person or people in charge will carefully review your lease agreement and send you a written confirmation that reaffirms the terms you originally agreed on. Your current lease is honored until it expires.

You May Need to Open Up Your Space for Potential Buyers

When your rental property is up for sale, the owner's agent may ask your permission to schedule appointments for potential buyers to view your property in advance.

Here's how it usually works:

>> If you're in a smaller property with one to six units, your unit likely needs to be shown. The agent will discuss with you when these showings will occur.

>> If you're in a larger apartment building, you may not get individual notification; because buyers typically only view a few units, yours may not be on the list.

In most cases, your lease requires you to allow potential buyers access to your rental as long as they give you notice beforehand. Just so you know, the agent may suggest you tidy up your space before these viewings, so plan accordingly.

You don't have to be present during these buyer tours. In fact, leaving your place while they're happening is often better. This way, the tours can go more quickly, and the prospective buyers can explore the space comfortably.

Your Lease Terms and Rights Are Transferred with the Sale

When a rental property is sold, the new property owner holds your lease terms and rights.

For example, suppose your lease states that you're responsible for the upkeep of the front and rear gardens including cutting the grass. The previous owner let this slide and you would go consecutive months without any maintenance or landscaping. Then the sale is complete; the new owner walks the property and observes that the grass is overgrown. You receive a notice reminding you of your responsibility per your lease agreement to maintain the front and rear yards and keep the grass cut.

If after the sale you encounter any uncertainties or questions about your lease or how the new owners are interpreting it, don't hesitate to seek clarification. Reach out to the new owner's property manager or consult a qualified attorney specializing in real estate law or landlord-tenant relations.

You Receive a Notice of Ownership Transfer

The notice of transfer of ownership provides

>> The new owner's name or LLC

>> Contact information for either the owner directly or the property manager

>> Confirmation that they've transferred ownership

>> Information about paying your rent

TIP

Email, text, or call the person listed on the notice. Make them aware of your name and address or apartment number and confirm anything you need help understanding about the notice. Make sure you discuss their preferred payment options. (I discuss paying the rent as usual later in this chapter.)

You Can (and Should) Research the New Owner

A good practice is to research the incoming landlord. Doing so can alert you to other properties they may own, and then you can find out about other tenants' experiences with the landlord. I always suggest this idea to tenants as a way to help them get comfortable with the new owner's style and temperament.

This research may ease any anxiety you have around getting to know a new landlord. Alternatively, this may have the opposite effect should your research uncover any unfavorable incidents. The crucial point is learning more about who you'll be dealing with.

To gather details about the new owner, review the letter you received about the change in ownership (see the preceding section) for any contact details or names. For research purposes, you need the name of the entity that owns the property, the property's address (which you probably already have, of course), and any other information that can help identify the new owner.

Then check online property records, which you can find on your county's or city's website. These records may provide information about the new owner, including their name and contact information.

You can then use that info to search for the new owner both through a search engine and on social media platforms. They may have a website, LinkedIn profile, or other online information that provides insights into their background and real estate portfolio.

Your Security Deposit Transfers to the New Owner

TIP

The security deposit you provided at the lease signing (see Chapter 6) is transferred to the new owner. I recommend documenting the deposit amount and payment date in your lease agreement; this kind of clear record-keeping helps prevent any misunderstandings down the line.

The new owner is still accountable for returning your security deposit according to the lease terms and local requirements. For tips on maximizing your chances of getting the full deposit back when you move out, check out Chapter 11.

You Can Ask About Capital Improvements for the Building

After the sale is successfully finalized, now is an excellent time for you to contact the new owner to ask about any capital improvements and other plans the owner has in mind.

Capital improvements require additional cash and repairs that, in most cases, are passed on to the tenants through increased rents. Things like a new roof, a spiffy new laundry room, touch-ups, and new lighting in the common area can increase the appeal and demand for the property. When you know what the landlord has in mind, you can prepare beforehand.

REMEMBER

Staying proactive by maintaining open lines of communication during this period can give you the essential information you need for a hassle-free tenancy under the new ownership.

You Must Pay the Rent as Usual

Upon the sale of the rental, you receive updated rent payment information, including options to pay electronically, by check, or by credit card. Management companies now use secure portals where you can enter your bank or credit card details to make rent payments easily. Some landlords also accept Venmo, Cash App, and other forms of electronic payment.

TIP

A property sale isn't an excuse to miss your rent payments, so whatever is the most convenient and stress-free way for you to pay rent, follow that path. If you're busy and forgetful, signing up for autopay may be your best option. If you prefer to send a check, make sure you put it in the mail well before it's due to allow flexibility to deal with postal delays. Find out more about paying rent on time in Chapter 6.

Chapter **15**

Nearly Ten Questions About Government Subsidies and Your Rent

Now more than ever, housing assistance is definitely needed as property values and rents have increased exponentially.

This chapter delves into government rental subsidies, such as Section 8 vouchers and other assistance programs. I explore who qualifies for these subsidies and provide insights into the available assistance.

For general information on rental assistance from the U.S. government, check out www.hud.gov/topics/rental_assistance.

What Is Section 8?

Section 8, previously known as the *Section 8 Housing Choice Voucher Program*, is a government-funded program run by the U.S. Department of Housing and Urban Development (HUD).

REMEMBER

Section 8's focus and intention are to help tenants find and pay for affordable housing (whether that's single-family homes, apartments, or townhomes) in the United States. The program provides monthly assistance to many American households struggling to pay rent.

TIP

Contact your local Public Housing Authority (PHA) or HUD location to find out more about this program. Visit www.hud.gov/program_offices/public_indian_housing/pha/contacts.

Who Qualifies for Section 8 Vouchers?

The local PHA determines the eligibility for a housing voucher based on a family's size and total yearly *gross* (pretax) income. As of this writing, a family's income can't be more than 50 percent of the median income for the county or metropolitan area where the family chooses to live. It's open to United States citizens and to noncitizens who have immigration status.

The median income for a Section 8 renter involves looking at the specific income limits that HUD sets for the geographic area. These income limits are regularly updated, and housing authorities use them to determine eligibility and rental assistance amounts for Section 8 participants. See www.huduser.gov/portal/datasets/il.html.

REMEMBER

By law, a PHA is required is give 75 percent of available vouchers to applicants whose incomes don't exceed 30 percent of the area median income. HUD publishes the median income levels by location; the PHA that serves the community you're searching in can provide you with the income limits for the area and family size.

What's the Application Process?

HUD collects your income and other information to determine your eligibility, the appropriate rental size, and the amount you'll contribute toward your rent and utilities. (I cover tallying your contribution in more detail in the following section.)

REMEMBER

The verification process plays a crucial role in determining eligibility and the level of assistance in the program. During this process, applicants are responsible for verifying various aspects, including income, assets, expenses, deductions, and any circumstances that may impact family eligibility or the amount of assistance provided.

When determining the annual combined income to qualify for the voucher, PHAs use the following specific criteria:

1. **Identify all the members of the household.**

2. **Calculate the total income for the head of the home, the co-head (if applicable), and any family members 18 or older.**

    This calculation is the foundation for assessing the household's income for eligibility and program considerations.

REMEMBER

Applicants and their families must sign consent forms to facilitate this verification process. These forms permit the collection of the necessary information to verify eligibility, income, assets, expenses, and deductions. Any applicant who doesn't consent isn't eligible to receive program benefits.

Additionally, family members 6 and older must submit their Social Security numbers as part of the verification process. Anyone who doesn't have a Social Security number has to certify that they've never been issued one.

How Does the PHA Calculate a Tenant's Contribution?

The local PHA determines the amount a family or individual must pay based on a sample of moderately priced rentals in the desired area.

The voucher covers the *payment standard*, which is 30 percent of the adjusted monthly gross income. If a tenant selects a rental whose rent exceeds the payment standard, they're responsible for covering the additional cost. If you're in this situation, make sure you consistently make payments on time.

REMEMBER

By law, a tenant is protected from paying more than 40 percent of their adjusted monthly income for rent when they relocate to a new unit where the rent surpasses the payment standard.

REMEMBER

The PHA's payment standard doesn't dictate a landlord's rent. Instead, it allows tenants to compare their means to the rents on potential properties.

How Does the Waiting List Work?

Because the demand for housing assistance usually exceeds the resources available to HUD and the neighborhood housing agencies, you can expect long waiting periods. In fact, a PHA may close its waiting list when it has more families than it can assist.

PHAs may establish local preferences for selecting applicants from their waiting lists based on the community's housing needs and priorities. For example, PHAs may give a priority to families who are

>> Homeless or living in substandard housing

>> Paying more than 50 percent of their income for rent

>> Involuntarily displaced (for example, the building you're living in requires a renovation or demolition, therefore requiring the tenants to be displaced)

Families who qualify for any such local preferences move ahead of other families on the list who don't.

Which Landlords Accept Section 8 Vouchers?

REMEMBER

Some states require property owners to take Section 8 vouchers, while others don't. In the latter case, a landlord or property management company can decide whether to accept Section 8 vouchers.

Property owners wanting to participate in the Section 8 program must adhere to specific housing standards (Housing Quality Standards, or HQS) established by HUD. These standards require that the property undergo inspection at least once a year throughout the tenancy to ensure that it complies in the following categories:

>> Sanitary facilities (also known as the bathroom)

>> Food preparation and refuse (trash) disposal

>> Space and security

>> Thermal environment (heating)

>> Illumination and electricity

>> Structure and materials (structural soundness and maintenance)

>> Interior air quality

>> Water supply

>> Lead-based paint

>> Access

>> Site and neighborhood

>> Sanitary condition

>> Smoke detectors

For HUD's full explanation of the HQS, check out www.hud.gov/sites/documents/DOC_35620.PDF.

Does a Section 8 Voucher Expire?

A PHA determines its voucher's expiration date, which you can find on the form. The expiration dates can range from 45 to 60 days from the date the voucher was issued. However, keep in mind the dates vary by state. You can call the PHA at 1-800-955-2232 to find out more about this.

Tenants must submit their rental applications for approval within this time frame unless the PHA grants an extension. Extensions are at the PHA's discretion and can be based on the conditions of the housing market and the effort the tenant has put into find a unit within the original voucher time frame.

How Do You Find Spaces Available to Rent with Section 8?

TIP

After completing the verification process and receiving approval, the next step is finding an apartment that accepts your housing voucher. Finding affordable apartments can be challenging, but here are some guidelines:

» **Online rental listing websites:** You can use sites like homes.com, trulia.com, or rent.com. In the search field, enter "income restricted" to filter results to properties that may accept housing vouchers.

» **Contact property managers or listing agents:** Mention that you've been approved for a housing voucher, ask whether the property is eligible, and discuss the application process.

» **HUD's website:** Search the official HUD website at hud.gov, where you can access listings of apartments participating in the Public Housing Voucher program. This site provides valuable information on available apartments and eligibility requirements.

» **Local nonprofit organizations:** Reach out to local nonprofit housing organizations specializing in subsidy and low-income housing. They have insights on available units and can assist you in your search.

» **General internet search:** Searching your favorite engine for "Housing Choice Voucher rentals" in your area can lead you to additional listings and resources.

Are There Rental Assistance Programs for Veterans?

Veterans can access rental subsidies by connecting with the HUD-Veterans Affairs Supportive Housing Program (HUD-VASH). The service is the combined effort of HUD and the Department of Veterans Affairs (VA) to offer veterans housing assistance similar to Section 8 benefits.

TIP

If you want more information about this opportunity and your eligibility, contact HUD or the VA for details and information. Start your research at www.hud.gov/program_offices/public_indian_housing/programs/hcv/vash and www.va.gov/homeless/hud-vash.asp.

Chapter **16**

Almost Ten Things a Rental Agent Can Do for You

Sure, you can look for a rental yourself, but why not consider hiring a rental agent? In a competitive rental market, having an agent by your side can make all the difference in securing your ideal home.

You can get the nitty-gritty on working with a rental agent in Chapter 4, but in this chapter, I discuss (nearly) ten ways one can help you during your search for a new home.

REMEMBER

Your dedicated agent not only eliminates the uncertainties from your rental search but also serves as your advocate, committed to guiding you in discovering your ideal home.

Sharing Market Expertise

When you hire a rental agent, you get to work with an expert who understands the local market and prices. The rental agent facilitates access to your preferred properties and to vetted landlords, and that professional guidance gives you an advantage.

Rental agents who are in tune with the nuances of the local market trends, pricing dynamics, and neighborhood intricacies play a vital role in helping renters secure their ideal homes at the most favorable terms. This expertise is the foundation for informed decision making, an in with the best properties for rent, and ensuring that all parties navigate the rental process confidently and efficiently. The rental agent ultimately fosters successful and mutually beneficial rental experiences.

Accessing the Best Listings for You

A rental agent's primary objective is to streamline your property search. Rental agents leverage their extensive networks — including clients, landlords, property managers, investors, and cooperating real estate agents — to provide access to the most suitable properties within your designated price range. This approach saves you valuable time during your home search and personalizes the process according to your preferences for amenities and features whenever possible. Collaborating with an agent can often get you an early look at your preferred listings.

REMEMBER

When you hire an agent, you're empowering your search. You owe it to yourself to work with a professional who puts your success above all.

Being a Neighborhood Expert

Rental agents are not only experts in their areas of operation but also passionate advocates for these communities they live and work in. They can provide valuable insights into a wide range of local aspects, including top-rated activities, parks, restaurants, shops, and their personal favorites in the neighborhood.

This wealth of information enhances your understanding of the area and helps you make more informed decisions about the rental you'll call home.

Negotiating on Your Behalf

When you're negotiating, an agent who's mastered the art of negotiating and has a solid understanding of pricing is worth their weight in gold. Here's what to look for:

>> **Expert negotiator:** A skilled rental agent is well-versed in the art of negotiation to help you get the best possible rent rate, lease term, included amenities, and so on.

>> **Tailored strategy:** A good agent adjusts their negotiation strategy to your specific needs and desires. They work to align the rental terms with your unique requirements.

>> **Impartial viewpoint:** Agents provide an objective perspective during negotiations, helping you make rational decisions based on market data rather than emotions.

TIP

By allowing your agent to conduct negotiations on your behalf, you save time and remove the stress of dealing with the landlord directly. Your agent handles the back-and-forth discussions and paperwork.

REMEMBER

An expert agent's negotiation skills and market expertise significantly impact your renting experience, maximizing your chances of securing favorable lease terms and minimizing the associated stress and indecisiveness.

Connecting You to Their Professional Network

A good rental agent knows the importance of building strong contacts with reputable landlords, property managers, and other agents to ensure that the flow of business is smooth. An agent's well-established network connects them to an extensive range of listings, including those not publicly advertised. (I discuss these pocket listings later in this chapter.) This inside scoop expands your rental options significantly.

For example, agents often receive early notifications from land-lords and property managers about new listings or expiring leases. They can pass this information on to their clients (namely, you), giving you priority access to viewings.

Guiding You Through the Rental Process

Prospective renters contact me about where and how to start their searches. When you hire a rental agent, one of the essential functions they add is quickly bringing you up to speed with the entire rental process. Whether they're meticulously identifying properties that align with your lifestyle or helping you assemble a stellar rental application, a rental agent enhances your quality of life by saving you valuable time and getting you back to your routine as quickly and efficiently as possible.

Adding Valuable Assessment Skills

Skilled rental agents go beyond being able to provide information and access; they add value through their ability to assess properties accurately, evaluate pricing dynamics, and consider variables that impact your rental experience. Their insights help you gauge a property's value and evaluate its suitability for your unique needs and preferences.

Letting You Know About Pocket Listings

TIP

Off-market listings, often called *pocket listings* or *whisper listings,* present an excellent opportunity to secure your next home in a highly competitive rental market. Even though these listings aren't being publicly advertised on mainstream real estate websites, agents with privileged access to these properties can easily find them. When you explore these word-of-mouth listings, you view a property with fewer eyes on it, creating a more comfortable and less competitive viewing experience.

TECHNICAL STUFF

Property owners opt for pocket listings for various reasons, including privacy concerns and a desire to test the rental waters before making a formal listing. This approach gained popularity in response to intense year-round competition in the rental market.

To tap into the benefits of off-market rental listings, renters should work closely with experienced rental agents with the insider knowledge and connections required to tap into these exclusive opportunities.

Providing Detailed Data

When you hire a rental agent for your rental search, you're not just securing a place, you're connecting to a wealth of professional expertise. Your agent serves as your data hub, providing transparent details about the property you may not have access to without an agent. This data includes crucial information such as the property's ownership history, construction date, amenities, previous rental rates, and other pertinent details.

As part of this service, you can expect to receive digital marketing materials and video tours that showcase the unique features of potential homes, further enhancing your search experience.

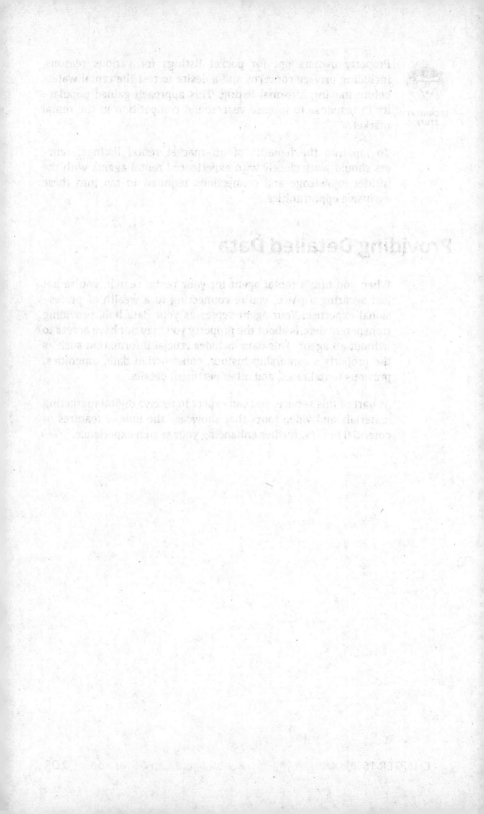

Index

About the Author

Abdul Muid, the visionary behind Ivey North, is a highly accomplished New York City real estate agent renowned for his strategic yet personalized approach to every facet of Manhattan and Brooklyn's home buying, selling, and rental process.

With over 15 years of experience and a career that boasts stellar achievements at two of the city's top residential firms, Corcoran and Compass, Abdul has consistently proven himself as a trusted, personable, and consummate professional. His impressive track record includes generating a remarkable $100 million sales volume. His expertise spans a broad spectrum, encompassing co-ops, condominiums, townhouses, investment properties, and land sales.

A native New Yorker, Abdul intimately understands the vibrant and diverse neighborhoods comprising Brooklyn and Manhattan. His journey into real estate was catalyzed by his profound love for the city and its ever-evolving landscape. Abdul thrives on the intangible benefits of life in New York City, starting his day with invigorating workouts and concluding it with culinary explorations at the city's latest dining establishments.

Beyond his professional endeavors, Abdul's abiding passion is real estate. He says, "I love waking up every day and doing what I love most. I am living my dream, meeting fantastic people daily, and representing some of the best homes in New York City."

Abdul's roots in a tight-knit Brooklyn family have instilled an unwavering commitment to uncompromising integrity, a strong work ethic, and a pursuit of excellence in his life and business. These attributes and his boundless energy and enthusiasm have earned him deep client loyalty, resulting in a thriving repeat and referral business. They also serve as the guiding principles on which he's building Ivey North.

When he's not tirelessly assisting his clients, Abdul relishes precious moments spent with his family, including his wife Ayanna, son Noah, daughter Ava, and the newest addition to his family, Asher. His zest for life extends to his love for working out, creating and running businesses, enjoying new restaurants, and traveling — particularly to his favorite cities and countries beyond New York: Lisbon, Porto, Paris, Los Angeles, Iceland, Morocco, and many others.

Dedication

I dedicate this book to anyone living their dream and appreciating the journey of life.

Author's Acknowledgments

Thanks to the Most High, the beginning and source of everything. To my parents for giving birth to my life. To Ayanna, whose timely challenges have pushed me to grow. To my children, whose unwavering inspiration keeps me moving forward.

I want to thank Jennifer Yee, Senior Acquisitions Editor at Wiley, who extended this incredible opportunity and was my guiding light of positive energy throughout this process. I want to thank Vicki Adang for her invaluable template training and Georgette Beatty, the phenomenal editor who skillfully kept me on track. Thank you to Kristie Pyles.

To all my clients, your unwavering support and words of encouragement have been a driving force. And to all the renters I've had the privilege of assisting, your trust means the world to me. Thank you.

Publisher's Acknowledgments

Senior Acquisitions Editor:
Jennifer Yee

Development Editor:
Georgette Beatty

Copy Editor: Megan Knoll

Technical Editors: Teri Lee,
Dave Omach

Production Editor:
Tamilmani Varadharaj

Cover Image: © PM Images/
Getty Images

Leverage the power

Dummies is the global leader in the reference category and one of the most trusted and highly regarded brands in the world. No longer just focused on books, customers now have access to the dummies content they need in the format they want. Together we'll craft a solution that engages your customers, stands out from the competition, and helps you meet your goals.

Advertising & Sponsorships

Connect with an engaged audience on a powerful multimedia site, and position your message alongside expert how-to content. Dummies.com is a one-stop shop for free, online information and know-how curated by a team of experts.

- Targeted ads
- Video
- Email Marketing
- Microsites
- Sweepstakes sponsorship

20 MILLION PAGE VIEWS EVERY SINGLE MONTH

15 MILLION UNIQUE VISITORS PER MONTH

43% OF ALL VISITORS ACCESS THE SITE VIA THEIR MOBILE DEVICES

700,000 NEWSLETTER SUBSCRIPTIONS TO THE INBOXES OF

300,000 UNIQUE INDIVIDUALS EVERY WEEK

# of dummies

Custom Publishing

Reach a global audience in any language by creating a solution that will differentiate you from competitors, amplify your message, and encourage customers to make a buying decision.

- Apps
- Books
- eBooks
- Video
- Audio
- Webinars

Brand Licensing & Content

Leverage the strength of the world's most popular reference brand to reach new audiences and channels of distribution.

For more information, visit **dummies.com/biz**

PERSONAL ENRICHMENT

Staying Sharp
9781119187790
USA $26.00
CAN $31.99
UK £19.99

Facebook
9781119179030
USA $21.99
CAN $25.99
UK £16.99

Guitar
9781119293354
USA $24.99
CAN $29.99
UK £17.99

Investing
9781119293347
USA $22.99
CAN $27.99
UK £16.99

Beekeeping
9781119310068
USA $22.99
CAN $27.99
UK £16.99

Digital Photography
9781119235606
USA $24.99
CAN $29.99
UK £17.99

Meditation
9781119251163
USA $24.99
CAN $29.99
UK £17.99

Pregnancy
9781119235491
USA $26.99
CAN $31.99
UK £19.99

Samsung Galaxy S7
9781119279952
USA $24.99
CAN $29.99
UK £17.99

iPhone
9781119283133
USA $24.99
CAN $29.99
UK £17.99

Crocheting
9781119287117
USA $24.99
CAN $29.99
UK £16.99

Nutrition
9781119130246
USA $22.99
CAN $27.99
UK £16.99

PROFESSIONAL DEVELOPMENT

Windows 10
9781119311041
USA $24.99
CAN $29.99
UK £17.99

AutoCAD
9781119255796
USA $39.99
CAN $47.99
UK £27.99

Excel 2016
9781119293439
USA $26.99
CAN $31.99
UK £19.99

QuickBooks 2017
9781119281467
USA $26.99
CAN $31.99
UK £19.99

macOS Sierra
9781119280651
USA $29.99
CAN $35.99
UK £21.99

LinkedIn
9781119251132
USA $24.99
CAN $29.99
UK £17.99

Windows 10
9781119310563
USA $34.00
CAN $41.99
UK £24.99

SharePoint 2016
9781119181705
USA $29.99
CAN $35.99
UK £21.99

Fundamental Analysis
9781119263593
USA $26.99
CAN $31.99
UK £19.99

Networking
9781119257769
USA $29.99
CAN $35.99
UK £21.99

Office 2016
9781119293477
USA $26.99
CAN $31.99
UK £19.99

Office 365
9781119265313
USA $24.99
CAN $29.99
UK £17.99

Salesforce.com
9781119239314
USA $29.99
CAN $35.99
UK £21.99

Coding
9781119293323
USA $29.99
CAN $35.99
UK £21.99

dummies.com

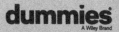

dummies
A Wiley Brand

Learning Made Easy

ACADEMIC

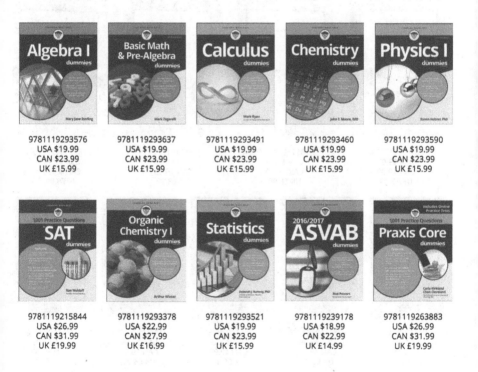

Algebra I dummies
Mary Jane Sterling
9781119293576
USA $19.99
CAN $23.99
UK £15.99

Basic Math & Pre-Algebra dummies
Mark Zegarelli
9781119293637
USA $19.99
CAN $23.99
UK £15.99

Calculus dummies
Mark Ryan
9781119293491
USA $19.99
CAN $23.99
UK £15.99

Chemistry dummies
John T. Moore, EdD
9781119293460
USA $19.99
CAN $23.99
UK £15.99

Physics I dummies
Steven Holzner, PhD
9781119293590
USA $19.99
CAN $23.99
UK £15.99

1001 Practice Questions SAT dummies
Ron Woldoff
9781119215844
USA $26.99
CAN $31.99
UK £19.99

Organic Chemistry I dummies
Arthur Winter
9781119293378
USA $22.99
CAN $27.99
UK £16.99

Statistics dummies
Deborah J. Rumsey, PhD
9781119293521
USA $19.99
CAN $23.99
UK £15.99

2016/2017 ASVAB dummies
Rod Powers
9781119239178
USA $18.99
CAN $22.99
UK £14.99

Includes Online Practice Tests 1001 Practice Questions Praxis Core dummies
Carla Kirkland Chan Cleveland
9781119263883
USA $26.99
CAN $31.99
UK £19.99

Available Everywhere Books Are Sold

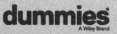

Small books for big imaginations

GETTING STARTED WITH Coding
9781119177173
USA $9.99
CAN $9.99
UK £8.99

MODDING Minecraft
9781119177272
USA $9.99
CAN $9.99
UK £8.99

MAKING YouTube VIDEOS
9781119177241
USA $9.99
CAN $9.99
UK £8.99

DESIGNING Digital Games
9781119177210
USA $9.99
CAN $9.99
UK £8.99

GETTING STARTED WITH Raspberry Pi
9781119262657
USA $9.99
CAN $9.99
UK £6.99

EXPERIMENTING WITH Science
9781119291336
USA $9.99
CAN $9.99
UK £6.99

CREATING Digital Animations
9781119233527
USA $9.99
CAN $9.99
UK £6.99

GETTING STARTED WITH Engineering
9781119291220
USA $9.99
CAN $9.99
UK £6.99

WRITING Computer Code
9781119177302
USA $9.99
CAN $9.99
UK £8.99

Unleash Their Creativity

dummies.com

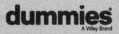